Key *for Key*

The Making of the United Kingdom

Robert Unwin

Stanley Thornes (Publishers) Ltd

The author would like to acknowledge the invaluable contribution of his wife, Pat, without whom this book would not have been possible.

A big 'thank you' for the professionalism, care and high standards of Barry Page and his team at Stanley Thornes, with whom it has been a pleasure to work: Hilary Norman (designer), Sophie Goldsworthy (copy editor) and Julia Hanson (picture research). And to Judith Harvey who commissioned the book.

Printed and bound in China by Midas

Acknowledgements

The authors and publishers are grateful to the following for permission to reproduce illustrations and photographs in this book.

Bridgeman Art Library, London: 12b Lucas de Heere The Family of Henry VIII Sudeley Castle, Glos., 18t National Maritime Museum, London, 23t Elizabeth I Armada Portrait Private Coll., 42b P.F. Poole Visitation & Surrender of Syon Nunnery to the Commissioners, 1539 City of Bristol Museum & Art Gallery, 49t Attempted Arrest of 5 Members of the House of Commons by Charles I, 1642 House of Lords, Westminster, London, 54t Houses of Parliament, London, 63 Dirck Stoop Coronation Procession of Charles II Museum of London, 69 Waggoner Fire of London, 1666 Guildhall Art Gallery, Corporation of London, 84–5 English School (16th Century) William Brooke, 10th Lord Cobham and his Family, 1567 Longleat House Wiltshire, 88 G, van Tilborg The Tichborne Dole, 1670 Tichborne Park, Hampshire, 94b Cottage Industry British Library, London, 99 English School (18th Century) Bristol Docks & Quay City of Bristol Museum & Art Gallery, 100 Hans Holbein Henry VIII Thyssen-Bornemisza Collection, 101 Van Dyck Charles I National Gallery, London, 102 Whitehall, London, 103t Marcus Gheeraerts the Younger Queen Elizabeth Dancing with Robert Dudley, Earl of Leicester Private Collection, 103b Jacob Savery A Village Fair Phillips the International Fine Art Auctioneers, 105 Visscher Globe Theatre British Library, London, 107c Francis Hayman Cricket in the Artillery Ground Marylebone Cricket Club, London, 109t Robert Hannah William Harvey Demonstrating to Charles I his Theory of the Circulation of the Blood Royal College of Physicians, London;
Bodleian Library, Oxford 109b (MS Ashmole 971 f.76v);
British Library 60b;
British Museum 11, 25;
Governors of Christ's Hospital, Horsham 651;
Emmanuel College, Cambridge © The Master, Fellows and Scholars of Emmanuel College, Cambridge 14t;
Mary Evans Picture Library 43, 97;
Fotomas Index 14b, 33t, 47, 48, 58, 60t, 61, 82–3, 87, 90b, 107t;
Glasgow Museums: Art Gallery & Museum, Kelvingrove 77;
Michael Holford 98;
Hulton Getty 19, 32b, 33cl & cr, 36c, 51c, 52b, 56, 64t & b, 93, 94t, 106, 108;
Mansell Collection 4b, 16, 18c, 21, 24, 28, 31, 35, 36t & b, 37, 41, 45, 49c, 50, 51t, 52t, 53, 54b, 59r & l, 62, 65r, 67, 70, 74, 75, 76, 81, 86, 91, 92, 95, 104t & b, 111;
Mirror Syndication International 44;
Museum of London 66;
The Trustees of the National Library of Scotland & Sir David Ogilvy, Bart 6;
National Maritime Museum, London 23b;
National Portrait Gallery, London 5t & c, 20, 29, 30, 39, 49tl, 72–3;
Private Collection 15;
The Royal Collection © HM the Queen 8t & b, 9, 12t;
By Permission of the President and Council of the Royal Society 110;
St. John's College, Cambridge 32t;
Sheldonian Theatre, University of Oxford/Thomas Photos 71r;
Spectrum Colour Library 711, 90t.

Every effort has been made to contact copyright holders and we apologise if any have been overlooked.

Contents

Crown and Parliament under the Tudors

The Tudor monarchs

Source A Family tree: the Houses of Lancaster and York

- **Who were the Tudors?**
- **How did the Tudors come to rule the country?**

Some periods in history are known by the names of the family of kings and queens who ruled at that time. For example, we use the word **Tudor** to describe that period of history, between 1485 and 1603, when the Tudor family of kings and queens ruled the country. This chapter is about the power of the **monarch** and about **Parliament**.

The Tudors, who ruled between 1485 and 1603, came from a family of Welsh landowners. During the **Wars of the Roses**, when the **Lancastrians** and the **Yorkists** fought over who was to be king, the Tudor family fought on the side of the Lancastrians. At the battle of Bosworth in 1485, the Yorkist King Richard III was killed. Henry Tudor, who had a claim to the throne, won the battle. He was made king, as Henry VII. He was the first of the Tudor rulers.

Source B The victory of Henry Tudor at the battle of Bosworth Field 1485

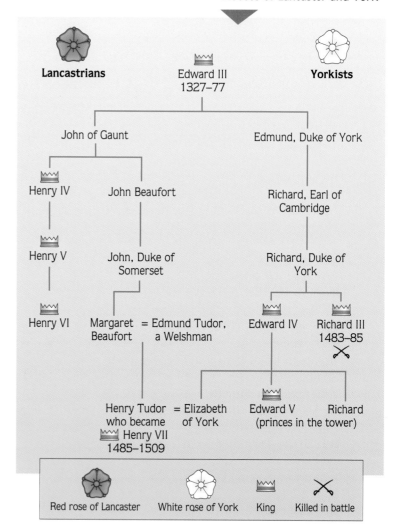

Source C Proclamation of Henry VII, 25 August 1485

The king ascertaineth [tells] you that Richard, Duke of Gloucester, late called King Richard, was slain at a place called Sandford within the shire of Leicester, and brought dead off the field into the town of Leicester, and there laid openly, that every man might see and look upon him.

How was the country ruled?

In many European countries at this time, the power of kings and queens was growing. In England the power of the nobles (great landowners) had been weakened by the Wars of the Roses. When Henry VII became king he wanted to make himself a strong and powerful ruler. His character was important in helping him to do this. He was strict, crafty and greedy. To increase his own power he made the nobles less powerful. He destroyed their castles and passed a law to stop the nobles having private armies. Those nobles who broke Henry's law were put on trial in a **court** called the **Court of the Star Chamber**. Under Henry VII taxes were collected more efficiently. Although he did not make great changes in the way the country was governed, he did make sure that **government** worked better.

How did the Tudors try to make sure their family kept the throne?

Henry VII did not have a strong family claim to the English throne. However, his victory at the battle of Bosworth, and the fact that the country was tired of the wars between the nobles, meant that most people accepted Henry as king. His marriage to Elizabeth of York also strengthened his position. However, during Henry's **reign** a number of **imposters** tried to claim the **crown**. One of these was Lambert Simnel who pretended to be Richard III's nephew. Simnel and his supporters were defeated by Henry at the battle of Stoke in 1487. A more dangerous threat came from Perkin Warbeck. Warbeck said he was one of the princes who had disappeared in the Tower during Richard III's reign. Warbeck's **rebellion** was also defeated. The defeat of these imposters strengthened Henry's position as king.

Source D Portrait of King Henry VII by Michiel Sittow, 1505

Source E Portrait of Elizabeth of York, the wife of Henry VII, artist unknown

Key words

Tudor The name of the family of kings and queens who ruled England between 1485 and 1603.

Monarch A king or queen. A country ruled by a king or a queen is called a monarchy.

Parliament Group of people who meet to make laws.

Wars of the Roses The civil wars in the fifteenth century between the Yorkists and the Lancastrians.

Lancastrians Those who supported the House of Lancaster in the Wars of the Roses.

Yorkists Those who supported the House of York in the Wars of the Roses.

Court The place where law and justice are carried out.

Court of the Star Chamber A room in the royal palace at Westminster with stars on the ceiling. Used as a court to try cases affecting the Crown. It became more important in Tudor and early Stuart times in increasing the power of the monarch. The Court of the Star Chamber was abolished in 1641.

Government The people with the power to rule a country.

Reign Period of time that a monarch rules.

Imposters People who pretend to be someone else.

Crown The monarchy (that is, the king or queen).

Rebellion An armed struggle by the people against a monarch or government.

Investigations

1 Look at the family tree (Source **A**). The Lancastrians and the Yorkists came from the same king. Who was he?

2 Look at Sources **B** and **C**. Who won the battle of Bosworth? Which Yorkist king was killed in the battle?

3 A legend says that, when Richard III was killed, the crown of England was found in a thorn bush. Has the artist who produced Source **B** shown any evidence of the legend in the picture?

4 By using the family tree and the text, explain how Henry Tudor became King Henry VII.

5 Read Source **C**. Why did the new king, Henry VII, order that the body of Richard III should be put on show for everyone to see?

How did Henry VII make friends with other countries?

Henry wanted to make friends with the rulers of other countries. He therefore planned marriages between his own family and other royal families. Henry's eldest son, Arthur, married Catherine of Aragon, the daughter of the king of Spain, in 1502. However, Arthur died later the same year. Henry VII then planned for Arthur's widow, Catherine, to marry his second son (also called Henry). Henry VII's daughter, Margaret, was married to King James IV of Scotland. This brought a short period of peace to the north of Britain (page 11). The marriages of Henry VII's children helped him to make powerful friends.

Lifeline: James IV King of Scotland

1473 Born
1488 James IV becomes King of Scotland
1495 Aberdeen University started
1496 Education Act leads to great improvements in Scottish schools
1511 Building of warship called *Great Michael*
1513 Death of James IV and many Scottish nobles at battle of Flodden Field

1470 — 1480 — 1490 — 1500 — 1510 — 1520

1502 Scotland and England make 'The Treaty of Perpetual Peace'
1503 Marriage to Margaret Tudor, daughter of Henry VII of England
1506 Royal College of Surgeons in Scotland started
1507 Royal charter to set up printing press in Scotland
1508 Scottish poetry printed

Source F Marriage of Henry VII's daughter, Margaret, and James IV King of Scotland

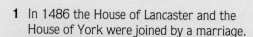

Investigations

1 In 1486 the House of Lancaster and the House of York were joined by a marriage.
   a) Can you name the Yorkist who married Henry VII?
   b) Why was the marriage a good idea? How did it make Henry VII a stronger king?

2 Use the text to answer the following questions:
   a) How did Henry VII overcome the nobles?
   b) How did Henry VII try to make his position as king secure?
   c) What else did Henry VII achieve as king?
   d) How did Henry VII use the royal marriages of his children to strengthen his position?
   e) When Henry VII died in 1509, who became king?

3 Look at Source **F**. It shows James IV carrying the standard (flag) of the Scottish kings (a lion rearing up on its hind legs). Margaret's costume shows the Royal Arms of England (three lions and the lilies or fleurs-de-lis which were used to show English claims to rule France). How has the artist used this information in showing the marriage of James IV of Scotland to Margaret Tudor in 1503?

4 This picture, showing a marriage in 1503, was painted one hundred years later, shortly before the death of Queen Elizabeth in 1603 (page 25). Why might that have been a good time to show a marriage between a Scottish king and an English princess?

5 When well-known people die, what they did in their lifetime is often written up. This is called an obituary. Write an obituary of King James IV of Scotland.

The four nations

> • **How were they ruled?**
> • **What were their emblems, badges and flags?**

The English, Scots, Welsh and Irish were the peoples of four separate and independent nations, each with their own language, history and culture. The peoples of Scotland, Ireland and Wales, who spoke the Gaelic and Welsh languages were descended from the Celtic peoples who had once controlled western Europe. Although there were different national identities within the British Isles, there were also important local and regional differences *within* each of the four nations.

Throughout the British Isles there was a rich variety of customs, dress, music, food and drink. Scotland had two native languages, the Gaelic-speaking Highlands and Islands, and the Scots-speaking Lowlands. Throughout the four nations, monarchs, noble families, towns, the Church and other groups of people used emblems, flags, badges and coats of arms to show their identity. These were widely used on portraits, costume, buildings and ships and helped to create a sense of belonging and loyalty.

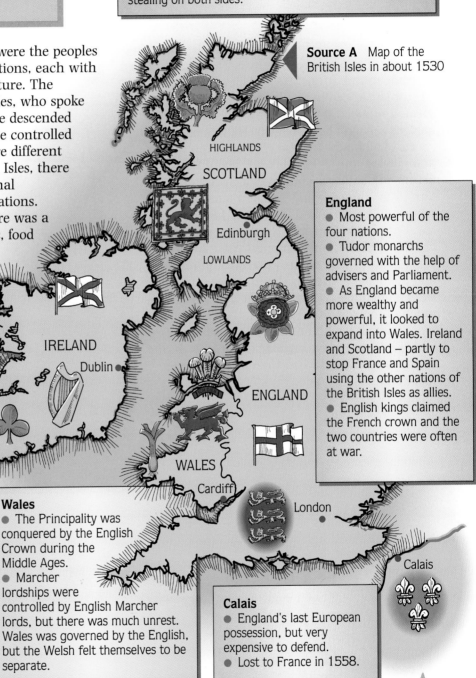

Scotland
● An independent kingdom ruled by the Stuart kings, with help from a council and the Scottish Parliament called the Three Estates.
● The power of the Scottish king was strongest in the Lowlands. In the Highlands, the clan chiefs had much local power.
● Scotland was often an ally of France against England. The Scottish-English border was lawless, with cattle-stealing on both sides.

Source A Map of the British Isles in about 1530

England
● Most powerful of the four nations.
● Tudor monarchs governed with the help of advisers and Parliament.
● As England became more wealthy and powerful, it looked to expand into Wales. Ireland and Scotland – partly to stop France and Spain using the other nations of the British Isles as allies.
● English kings claimed the French crown and the two countries were often at war.

Ireland
● An independent land with a rich Gaelic language and culture.
● English control was strongest in the 'Pale' – the area of land round Dublin. English kings were called 'lords of Ireland' but had little power outside the Pale.
● Irish (Gaelic) nobles valued their freedom.

Wales
● The Principality was conquered by the English Crown during the Middle Ages.
● Marcher lordships were controlled by English Marcher lords, but there was much unrest. Wales was governed by the English, but the Welsh felt themselves to be separate.

Calais
● England's last European possession, but very expensive to defend.
● Lost to France in 1558.

Investigations

1 Discuss how emblems, badges and flags are used today – for example at sporting occasions. How are they used to build up a sense of belonging and identity?

2 Collect and display examples of the use of emblems, badges, flags and coats of arms. (Examples include coins, stamps, inn (pub) signs.)

Henry VIII

> The King is the handsomest potentate [powerful ruler] I ever set eyes on, above the usual height, with an extremely fine calf to his leg, his complexion very fair and bright, with auburn hair combed straight and short, in the French fashion, and a round face so very beautiful that it would become a pretty woman, his throat being rather long and thick ... He speaks French, English, and Latin, and a little Italian; plays well on the lute and harpsichord, sings from a book at sight, draws the bow with greater strength than any man in England and jousts marvellously

What was Henry VIII like?

When Henry VII died in 1509 his son became king as Henry VIII. The new king was 18 years old when he came to the throne. He was clever but could also be ruthless in dealing with people. He could speak a number of foreign languages and enjoyed talking about religion. He was good at sports of all kinds. He also enjoyed composing and playing music. Henry knew about the artists and builders who were at work in the European countries and he spent a lot of money on building and improving his own royal palaces in England. He also supported artists and musicians. Amongst these was the artist Holbein who painted portraits of the king and members of the **royal court** (page 100). Henry's rich lifestyle meant that he soon spent much of the wealth left by his father. His failed marriages, ill health and a war in France which he was losing, made him unhappy. In his later years, in the 1540s, Henry became even more ruthless.

Source B
Henry VIII departs from Dover
(for the 'Field of the Cloth of Gold')

Source C The Field of the Cloth of Gold

Royal court The royal household and the servants who looked after the monarch.

Key words

How was the country governed under Henry VIII?

Henry VIII expected his **advisers** to do most of the day-to-day work of running the country. However, they had to obey the king. Henry's chief adviser from 1515 to 1527 was Thomas Wolsey, who held three important offices. He was **Archbishop** of York, **Chancellor** of England and a **Cardinal** in the **Roman Catholic Church**. Unfortunately for Wolsey, he got the blame when Henry's request for an **annulment** of his marriage to Catherine of Aragon was refused by the **Pope** in Rome. Also, the country was almost **bankrupt** under Wolsey, although this was partly due to Henry's quarrels with other countries. As a result Wolsey fell from power.

Another of Henry VIII's advisers was Thomas Cromwell. Cromwell was Henry's adviser when the king quarrelled with the Pope over the question of his divorce, and of his re-marriage to his second wife Anne Boleyn. Cromwell was also his adviser when the **monasteries** were closed (pages 38–9).

Source D   Henry VIII opening Parliament in 1523

Source E   Henry VIII on Parliament (1543)

> We are at our most royal when we come together with one Parliament as one body. Any threat to one part of the body is a threat to us all …

Key words

Advisers   People appointed to advise, that is to offer a view on what actions to take.
Archbishop   A chief bishop of an area or of a group of bishops within the Christian Church.
Chancellor   The most important adviser or minister of the king in Tudor times.
Cardinal   A person who holds a very high position in the Roman Catholic Church.
Roman Catholic Church   Christian Church with the Pope as its head.
Annulment   To cancel an agreement, for example a marriage.
Pope   The leader or head of the Roman Catholic Church.
Bankrupt   A person who is unable to pay his or her debts.
Monasteries   Places where groups of monks live a religious life.

Investigations

1   Look at Source **A**. Was the ambassador from Venice impressed by Henry VIII? Why was this?

2   What kinds of activities did Henry VIII enjoy? Would you say he was a talented man? How might the sort of man Henry was help him as king?

3   Look at Source **B**. Use the following information to write about the power of Henry VIII:
   • the fort – one of many built by Henry on the south coast;
   • the strong guns;
   • Henry standing on his flagship *Great Harry* (in the centre of the picture);
   a) Write about the ships, guns and forts to show that Henry was a powerful king.
   b) Why was Henry VIII in a strong position when he became king in 1509?

4   Source **C** shows the Field of Cloth of Gold where Henry VIII met Francis I, the King of France, for talks in 1520. How did the kings of different countries try to show their importance and power to each other and to their people?

5   Look at Source **D**. Who seems to be the most important person in Parliament? What ways has the artist used to make this person look the most powerful?

The expansion of England in the early sixteenth century

Why were England and Wales united?

By Tudor times, England, the Principality of Wales, the Lordship of Ireland and the Isle of Man were united (joined) under the English Crown. The power of the monarch was greatest in England, especially in London and the south-east. The further away from London, the less power the monarch had.

For centuries, Wales had been divided into two main regions. The lands in the east and south of Wales had been conquered by powerful lords after the Norman Conquest of England. These were the **Marcher lordships**. To the west of these was the Principality, that is those parts of Wales that had been conquered by the English king in the Middle Ages and ruled by the Prince of Wales.

The Tudor family came from Wales. They were proud of this. Some Welsh landowners were able to speak both Welsh and English. They were given positions at the English royal court. They wanted to do well in England, and to strengthen the ties between the two countries.

In Wales, cattle farming was important. Sometimes great lords, with their armed men, stole cattle from their neighbours. The Welsh law courts were not able to keep law and order. In the 1530s, the head of the Council for Wales, called Rowland Lee, tried to stop crime by the landowners in the Marcher lordships. However, despite harsh punishments, law breaking continued.

How were England and Wales united?

During the reign of Henry VIII, England and Wales were united by two Acts of Parliament. These Acts of Union were passed by Parliament in 1536 and 1543. They brought about important changes for Wales:
- Wales was divided into 13 counties (or shires), organised like English ones;
- The counties of Wales could elect MPs to the Parliament at Westminster;
- English law replaced Welsh law throughout Wales;
- Public officials had to use the English language and not Welsh.

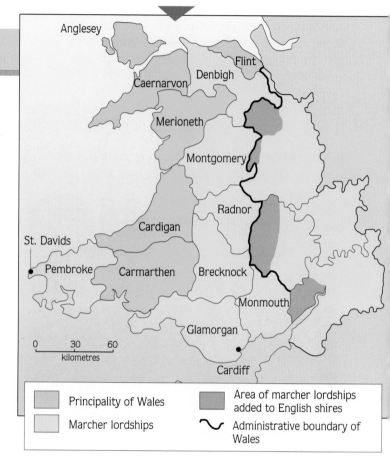

Source A Tudor Wales before and after the Union

Anglesey
Flint
Caernarvon
Denbigh
Merioneth
Montgomery
Radnor
Cardigan
St. Davids
Pembroke
Carmarthen
Brecknock
Monmouth
Glamorgan
Cardiff

0   30   60
kilometres

Principality of Wales	Area of marcher lordships added to English shires
Marcher lordships	Administrative boundary of Wales

What was Wales like after the Union?

After the Union, law and order improved in Wales. The cattle-thieves were punished. Welsh cattle drovers were able to walk their herds of animals more easily from the hill farms of Wales to markets in England, for example to London.

At first, the Acts of Union damaged Welsh culture. All Welsh officials were made to speak English. Parliament used the English language. Welsh gentlemen now looked on Welsh as a less important language, and some began to behave as if they were English. They married into English families, used English ways and sent their children to schools in England. However, the growth of the **Protestant** religion helped to keep the Welsh language in use (page 32).

Key words

Marcher lordships Areas controlled by lords or nobles on the borders of England and Wales.
Protestant Christians who broke away from the Roman Catholic Church at the Reformation.

How did the Tudors strengthen their power in Ireland?

The people of Ireland had a language and rich culture that dated back to **Celtic** times. In the early Tudor period, the English kings were still known as 'Lords of Ireland', a title that had been used for hundreds of years. However, they only controlled a small area around Dublin known as 'the Pale'. Outside the Pale, in the other parts of Ireland, the native Irish princes and the people were against being ruled from either England or Dublin. The language, culture and the old ways of life of the native Irish lived on in the mountains, woods and marshes of the country.

Peace in Ireland never lasted long. In the 1530s the Irish princes were in revolt. Thomas Cromwell decided to take action against the Irish rebels and to increase English power in Ireland. In 1540 Henry VIII made himself King of Ireland. Henry VIII also said he was head of the Church in Ireland and the monasteries in the Pale were closed down. This made relations between Protestant England and Catholic Ireland worse (pages 16–17).

Why were relations between England and Scotland difficult?

In the sixteenth century, Scotland was a separate country with its own royal family (the **Stuarts**) and its own Parliament in Edinburgh. The Scots and English were old enemies. Scotland often made **treaties** of friendship with France, the other old enemy of England. The marriage of Henry VIII's sister, Margaret, to King James IV of Scotland had brought peace. However, this peace did not last. When Henry VIII went to war with France, the Scots invaded England. The Scots were defeated at the battle of Flodden in 1513. King James IV of Scotland and many of the Scottish nobles were killed.

In the 1540s Henry VIII tried to conquer Scotland. Although the English won the battle of Solway Moss (1542) Henry never became king of Scotland.

Source B
Henry VIII's Royal Arms

Key words

Celtic The people who lived in Ireland, Wales, Scotland and Cornwall who came from the people who occupied much of Europe before the Romans. The Celts have distinct languages and way of life.

Stuarts The name of the family of kings and queens who ruled Scotland in the middle ages, and who became rulers of Scotland and England between 1603 and 1714.

Treaties Agreements between countries, sometimes following a disagreement or war.

Investigations

1 Look at Source **B**. Can you find:
- the arms of England (three lions walking);
- the fleurs-de-lis which show that the English king had a claim to the French throne;
- the English lion supporting the shield;
- the dragon of Wales supporting the shield?

2 Look at the emblems on modern coins. How do the Royal Arms of today differ from those of Henry VIII. Can you explain the difference between the Tudor emblems and those of the present day?

Henry VIII's successors

How did Henry VIII try to make sure that the Tudors kept the throne?

In 1540 Thomas Cromwell was beheaded. He fell from power partly because Henry was displeased by the way Cromwell had handled the king's marriage to his fourth wife, Anne of Cleves. In his later years Henry VIII became more concerned about the future of the Tudor family. Members of other families that could make a claim to the throne were often executed so that they were no longer a threat. One of the main reasons for Henry's six marriages was his wish for a male **heir** to succeed him on the throne. He wanted the Tudor line of monarchs to continue. However, when Henry died in 1547, he left only a weak and sickly son, Edward, to succeed him as heir. There were also two daughters, Mary and Elizabeth, by different marriages.

Source A The family of Henry VIII (1)

Source B
The family of
Henry VIII (2)

Key words

Heir A person who will become the next monarch. A person who, by law, receives property or a title on the death of the owner.

Edward VI and his Regents

Edward VI was the only son of Henry VIII and his third wife, Jane Seymour. He was only nine years old when he became king. A **Council** was set up to rule the country until Edward was old enough to rule it himself. The head of the Council (or the **Regent** as he was known) was the Duke of Somerset. In 1549 Somerset was overthrown and replaced by the Duke of Northumberland. By the 1550s it was clear that the boy king Edward VI had not long to live. Shortly before Edward's death, the Duke of Northumberland persuaded the young king to bar his two sisters, Mary and Elizabeth, from inheriting the throne. Instead, Northumberland wanted his own daughter-in-law, Lady Jane Grey, to become queen. However, Northumberland's plan to make Lady Jane Grey queen on Edward's death was defeated. In 1553, when Edward died, Mary, the eldest daughter of Henry VIII, was welcomed to London as the rightful Tudor queen. Lady Jane Grey, a girl of eighteen years of age, and a Protestant, had been recognised as queen for a few days only. She was imprisoned and later executed. In history she is known as the Nine Days Queen.

Mary I

Mary I was the daughter of Henry VIII and his first wife, Catherine of Aragon. When Henry had married his second wife, Anne Boleyn, Mary had been declared **illegitimate**. This meant that she was not recognised as his legal heiress. Later however, before Henry died, Mary's claim to the throne was recognised. She became queen in 1553 but soon became unpopular (pages 30–1).

Mary had been brought up as a **Roman Catholic**. She wanted the people of England to return to Roman Catholicism and began to **persecute** the Protestants. Mary's marriage to the Catholic King Philip II of Spain also caused difficulties. England had tried to stay out of European affairs. France and Spain were often at war with one another. Mary's marriage to the King of Spain meant that England became allied with (on the side of) Spain against France. Many people in England disliked the marriage. Sir Thomas Wyatt led a revolt against Mary but it was defeated.

In 1558, because of England's involvement in the war between Spain and France, England lost the important port of Calais. Calais had been the last English territory on the French mainland. The marriage of Mary and Philip failed to produce an heir to the throne. Thus, when Mary died in 1558, her half-sister Elizabeth became queen.

Key words

Council A group of people who meet to advise the monarch.
Regent A person who rules while the monarch is too young to do so.
Illegitimate A person whose parents were not lawfully married when they were born.
Roman Catholic A member of the Roman Catholic Church.
Persecute To ill treat someone or treat them unjustly because of their religious or political beliefs.

Investigations

1 Look at Sources **A** and **B**.
   a) One painting was made in 1545, the other around 1560. Can you say when each was painted?
   b) What differences can you see between the two paintings?

2 Which person is shown closest to the monarch and the throne in both paintings? Was this to show that:
   a) he was the youngest, b) he was the next heir to the throne, or c) he was the king's favourite?

3 a) Why do you think the artist painted the God of War close to Mary and Philip (Source **B**)?
   b) Why do you think the artist painted the Goddess of Plenty holding the hand of Elizabeth I?

4 Look at the time frame below. How does it help you to understand the paintings?

Date	Event
1538	Birth of Edward
1538	Death of Jane Seymour in childbirth
1547	Death of Henry VIII. Edward VI becomes king
1553	Death of Edward VI. Mary I becomes queen
1554	Marriage of Mary I and Philip II of Spain
1558	Death of Mary I. Elizabeth I becomes queen

5 What do you notice about the Royal Arms in each painting?

6 What work did the Regent and the Council have to do between 1547 and 1553?

7 Lady Jane Grey became known as the 'Nine Days Queen'. Why? Can you say what happened to her?

2 The Age of Elizabeth I

Elizabeth I

What was Elizabeth I like?

Elizabeth was the daughter of Henry VIII and his second wife, Anne Boleyn. She was born in 1533. She was well educated, and had a good knowledge of foreign languages. However she had lived in fear for most of her childhood. When her mother was executed, her father Henry VIII had declared Elizabeth illegitimate. During the reign of her sister, Mary I, Elizabeth had been held prisoner for a short time in the Tower of London. These difficulties meant that Elizabeth had to learn how to survive.

Elizabeth became queen in 1558 and reigned for 45 years. She was clever but vain. As queen, she wanted to win the loyalty and admiration of her subjects. She became very popular and people called her 'Gloriana'. Artists, writers, and musicians praised the queen in their work. Explorers wanted to do great things to please her and win her favour. Parliament wanted Elizabeth to marry but she never did.

Source B *The Faerie Queene* by Edmund Spenser

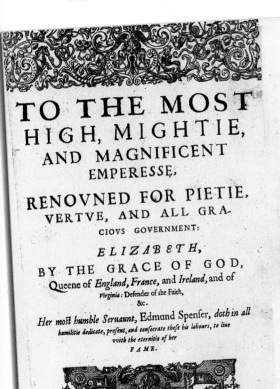

The Tudor royal court

The royal household, along with the servants who looked after the monarch, were known as the royal court. Many people were needed to serve the monarch and the court. The monarch had to be guarded. Secretaries were employed to deal with letters, and to keep accounts in order. A large staff was needed to look after visitors from all parts of the country and from abroad. The monarch and the household had to be fed. They also had to be kept entertained. Dances, plays and other amusements were organised indoors. Hunting and all kinds of outdoor sports were also popular.

The royal court was also the centre of government. It was here that important decisions were made by the monarch with the help of advisers. Elizabeth I was a strong leader and she often chose wise people to advise her. One of these advisers was Lord Burleigh. At court Elizabeth was clever enough to play off one group of courtiers against another to keep her position strong. Because Elizabeth had her favourites, some people were jealous and competed to get her attention. Courtiers who lost the queen's favour could be a danger. For example, in 1600 the Earl of Essex, who had been one of the queen's favourites, plotted against her. The plotters were overpowered and Essex was later executed.

What was a royal progress?

Monarchs often travelled about and stayed in different parts of the country. This was partly to save money by being entertained at the cost of rich **courtiers**. It was also to get the support of important nobles. The travels were known as royal **progresses**. Large numbers of the royal court travelled with the monarch. Elizabethan nobles competed with one another to provide the best entertainment for the queen. They often spent a lot of money on their houses and gardens and in planning entertainments in readiness for the queen's visit. The queen made many royal progresses during her reign, perhaps the most famous being to Kenilworth Castle in Warwickshire.

Source C Elizabeth I being carried by her courtiers (c.1600)

Investigations

1 Identify the main features in Source **A** by linking the numbers in the picture with the correct descriptions in the chart below. The first one is done for you.

Feature	Number
The crown and Tudor rose	2
The lion of England	
The dragon of Wales	
The fleur-de-lis and crown	
The orb in Elizabeth's right hand	
The sceptre in Elizabeth's left hand	

2 Does the picture show Elizabeth as a powerful or weak monarch? Say why you think this.

3 Source **B** shows the start of a poem called *The Faerie Queen*, written by Edmund Spenser. For whom did Spenser write the poem?

4 Write down the words Spenser used in the dedication (left-hand page) to praise Elizabeth. For example, MOST HIGH . . . Why do you think the poet praised the queen in this way?

5 Which countries did Elizabeth claim to rule over?

6 What did Spenser say about himself?

7 Use Source **C** and the information in the text.
   a) How is the queen being carried?
   b) In what other ways might she travel?

8 How has the artist shown the glamour and wealth of the Elizabethan Court surrounding the queen?

9 Which kind or *class* of people are shown with Elizabeth I? Are they merchants, labourers or nobles at Elizabeth's royal court ?

Key words

Courtiers People present at the royal court of a monarch.
Progresses Journeys or official tours usually made by the monarch.

The expansion of England

The Irish and English were separate peoples. Many Irish did not like the English and thought of them as foreigners in their country. Most English people did not understand the Irish, their language, or their ways of life. During the Tudor period, the English became more powerful in Ireland (page 11). They became more involved in farming, **trade**, the law and religion. The use of the English language spread more widely in Ireland. There was another reason why many Irish and English disagreed. England became a Protestant country, while most of the people in Ireland stayed Roman Catholic.

Source A   Extract from Polydore Vergil, *Anglicae Historiae* (1534–55)

I n all Ireland ... are only two sorts of men ... of which one is gentle and cultured. To these wealthier and more civilised inhabitants many of the merchants of neighbouring peoples come on business ... the English in particular ... these Irish easily acquire their manner of life and ... understood the language ... Such Irish all obey the English king. The other type of islander is savage ... and uncouth. From ... their primitive habits they are known as 'wild men of the woods'; but for all that they are good Christians. They have various rulers to whom they are subjected and who constantly fight among themselves. ... these Irishmen excel the others in ferocity, and – being more eager for revolutions – are found readier to support any type of upheaval.

Source B   Sketch from *Image of Ireland*, by John Derrick (1581)

Key words

Trade   The buying and selling of goods to make money.

16

Income in 1600	£ (extracts)	Expenditure in 1600	£ (extracts)
Taxes granted by Parliament	160,000	War in Ireland	320,000
Customs duties from ports	80,000	Pensions given by queen	26,000
Rents from people on queen's land	60,000	Help to Dutch rebels against Spain	25,000
Customs duties from wine	24,000	The navy	17,000
Payments from church taxes	20,000	Household expenses	8,000
Fines collected in the law courts	10,000	Payment for small private army	6,400
Fines against Catholics	7,000	Looking after castles and forts	6,000
Payments for giving trading licences	5,000	Looking after royal jewels and treasures	6,000
Sale of queen's lands	4,000	Looking after royal buildings	5,000
Payments from the Chancellor	4,000	Payments to servants	4,000
		Payments for courtiers' clothes	4,000
		Expenses for ambassadors	4,000
		Queen's personal spending	2,000
		Payment of judges	1,600
	374,000		435 000

When did the English plantations in Ireland begin?

During the reign of Mary I, English soldiers forced out a number of the Irish lords and gave their lands to English settlers. English farmers were 'planted' on Irish land and so began the plantations. Ireland became a **colony** of England.

Why and how was Ireland colonised?

During the reign of Elizabeth I, new plantations were set up in Ireland. This was partly because the English feared that the Spanish might use Ireland as a military base to invade England.

The Irish did not want to lose their land and they did not want to be ruled by the English. The Irish rebelled against the plantations and attacked the English settlers. The Irish revolts were put down harshly by English soldiers. After the defeat of each revolt, more of the lands of the Irish were taken from them and handed over to English Protestant settlers.

The most serious Irish revolt took place in Ulster in the 1590s. The Irish received some help from Spain. At first the Irish were successful. In the long term, however, the English army was stronger and many Irish lords were forced to surrender. By the end of Elizabeth's reign, the English had built forts in many parts of Ireland to keep order.

Investigations

1 Divide a page in your exercise book into two columns. Using the information in Source **A**, list the similarities and differences between the 'two sorts' of Irish people.

2 a) What did the author like about the 'first sort' of Irish people?
   b) Did he like anything at all about the 'second sort'?
   c) How did the author explain the differences between the two sorts of people?
   d) Do you think the author has given a one-sided (biased) view?

3 Look at Source **B**.
   a) Which 'sort' of Irish people does the sketch show?
   b) Write about the scene from a favourable point of view and give the sketch a favourable caption (title). Then write about it from an unfavourable point of view and give it an unfavourable title. Say how people might have different points of view about the lifestyle of another race.

4 What information does Source **C** give about the cost of the war in Ireland?

5 What was the main way of raising money to fight the war?

6 Why might a long war mean that Parliament had to be called to meet more often?

Key words

Colony Settlers and settlements in another country fully or partly under the rule of the country where the settlers came from.

The beginnings of overseas exploration

Source A Francis Drake's compass and sundial

How did the Tudors help trade and exploration?

The Tudor kings and queens wanted to increase the wealth of the country. Henry VII had got Parliament to pass the **Navigation Acts**. These were intended to help trade by using English ships to import and export goods. Henry also encouraged the overseas **explorations** of Sebastian and John Cabot to Newfoundland. Later, Elizabeth I supported some of the trading companies, for example the Muscovy Company, the Levant Company and the East India Company (page 98).

Sir Francis Drake

Elizabethan **explorers** sailed to many parts of the world. They wanted money and land for themselves. They also found new places for England to trade with. A famous Elizabethan **adventurer** was Francis Drake. Drake was born in Devon about 1540 and made many sea voyages. Between 1577 and 1580 he sailed round the world, plundering (attacking and robbing) Spanish and Portuguese ships as he did so. When he returned with a large amount of booty (treasure), Drake was **knighted** by Queen Elizabeth on board his ship, the *Golden Hind.*

Source B Contemporary picture celebrating Francis Drake's voyage round the world

Investigations

Key words

Navigation Acts Laws passed by Parliament setting out rules for ships, shipping and trade.
Explorations Travels to unknown or undiscovered places.
Explorers People who travel to unknown or undiscovered places.
Adventurer A person who sets out on a daring journey to gain riches, fame or enjoyment.
Knighted A title awarded by a monarch to a subject for service or achievement.

1 Look at Source **A**. How would an explorer or sailor use **a)** a compass, and **b)** a pocket sundial?

2 The picture in Source **B** shows: • a portrait of Francis Drake • his ship the *Golden Hind* • two maps of the globe.
   a) Explain why each of these features was included?
   b) If you could add one other feature what would it be, and why?

3 To the English, Francis Drake was a hero. How might the Spanish and Portuguese have described him?

Sir Walter Raleigh

Another explorer was Walter Raleigh who was born in Devon about 1552. He was for a time a favourite of the queen and wanted to please her by finding riches and new lands overseas. Raleigh explored parts of North America which he called 'Virginia', in honour of the 'Virgin Queen', Elizabeth I. It is said that he brought tobacco and potatoes back to England. In 1595 Raleigh went to Guyana in South America to look for gold. He sailed across the Atlantic Ocean. On the island of Trinidad, Raleigh destroyed the Spaniards' port of San Josef. Raleigh was looking for Manoa or Eldorado, a place said to be full of treasure, but he did not find it.

When James I became king in 1603, Raleigh fell from favour. He was put in prison for **treason** against the Crown. After twelve years in prison, Raleigh asked the king to let him go back to South America to find gold. In 1618 Raleigh returned to Guyana with his son to look for gold. Raleigh did not find gold and his son was killed. When Raleigh returned to England he was executed.

Source C An early advertisement for tobacco

Investigations

4 Look at Source **C** and say what you can learn from the advertisement. Consider the following in your answer:
 • What is tobacco? • What two climatic conditions are needed to grow it? • Who owned the land on which the tobacco was grown? • Why was he called a planter? • Who did the hard work on the plantation? • How was the tobacco stored?

5 Some of the ships shown were bringing black slaves. Where had the slaves been brought from? Why were they needed on the plantation?

6 Tobacco was originally valued as a medicine. What other use was soon found for it? What do we now know about tobacco which was not known in the sixteenth century?

Key words

Treason A crime against the monarch or the country.

Depth Study:
Threats to Elizabeth I and the war with Spain 1585–1604

Although Elizabeth I was a popular queen, there were a number of **uprisings** and **plots** against her. In 1569 some of the nobles of northern England rose up in rebellion against her. This uprising was defeated and the leaders were put to death. In 1583 a plot against the queen, led by Francis Throckmorton, was discovered. The uprisings and plots were partly caused by dislike of the growing power of the monarchy and government. There was also a wish, by some people, to return England to the old Catholic faith. Elizabeth's government employed secret agents to seek out those who might plot against her. There were always fears that the plotters might have the support of Spain, the most powerful Catholic country in Europe (page 27).

What were the causes of the war with Spain?

Elizabeth I and King Philip II of Spain were enemies. Elizabeth was a Protestant queen. Philip, who was the most powerful king in Europe, was a Roman Catholic. Philip wanted England to be ruled by a Catholic monarch again. There were a number of plots against Elizabeth. These included plots to put her cousin, Mary Queen of Scots, on the English throne. Mary was a Roman Catholic. She had been forced, by the Scots, to leave Scotland. While held captive in England, Mary was used in plots against Elizabeth. In 1587 Elizabeth reluctantly agreed to have Mary executed so that she would no longer be a threat to her.

Source A
Portrait of Mary Queen of Scots

Investigations

1 Look at Source **A**. How has the artist shown Mary as a Catholic queen?

2 Using the lifeline, select two separate years which were turning points in Mary's life. Explain your choices.

3 When Mary left Scotland in 1547 it was still a Catholic country. When she returned in 1561 it was becoming a Protestant country. How might this change have made difficulties for Mary?

4 Look at Source **B**. What can you see in the drawing at the points numbered 1, 2 and 3? Would you say that the people watching the execution were important people or ordinary people? Explain your answer.

Key words

Uprisings Rebellion or rising up of the people.
Plots Secret plans.

1542 Born – daughter of James V, Scottish king, and Mary of Guise (France) (Mary became Queen of Scotland on death of her father James V. Mary of Guise became Regent and governed in Scotland.)

1547 Mary sent to be educated as a Catholic in France

1557 Mary married French prince called Francis

1561 Mary returned to Scotland to reign as Scottish queen

1565 Mary's second marriage. Her husband is her cousin Lord Darnley

1567 Murder of Darnley, Mary's second husband. Mary married Lord Bothwell, probably one of Darnley's murderers. Scots rose in revolt against Mary – civil war – Mary forced to abdicate. Mary's son James becomes King of Scotland as James VI

1586 Babbington plot to kill Queen Elizabeth

1540 **1550** **1560** **1570** **1580** **1590**

1558 Francis becomes King of France. Mary is Queen of France and Scotland

1560 Death of Francis so Mary becomes a widow

1568 Mary fled to England to the protection of her cousin Queen Elizabeth. Mary kept in prison. Danger of being accused of plotting against Elizabeth.

1566 Murder of Mary's secretary, David Rizzio, on Darnley's orders. Birth of Mary's son James

1587 Mary's trial and execution at Fotheringay Castle

Source B The Execution of Mary Queen of Scots at Fotheringay Castle

A planned invasion

English adventurers and pirates often attacked King Philip of Spain's treasure ships as they sailed from the Spanish territories in the New World (that is, the Americas). Philip was also angry that Elizabeth was helping the Protestant people of the Netherlands (Holland) who were fighting to be free of Spanish and Catholic rule. He decided to invade England. However the launching of the Spanish invasion fleet was delayed for a year because Sir Francis Drake raided the Spanish port of Cadiz and set fire to many ships. In history this event became known as 'the singeing of the King of Spain's beard'.

21

How was the Spanish Armada defeated?

One of the main events of the war between England and Spain was the defeat of the Spanish **Armada**. In 1588 Philip II sent an Armada of ships to invade England. It was commanded by the Duke of Medina Sidonia. In May 1588 about 130 ships with 8000 sailors, 19,000 soldiers and more than 2000 cannon set sail from Lisbon. The Spanish plan was that the Armada would control the English Channel. Then it would be possible to bring over to England an army of Spanish and **mercenary** soldiers who were waiting in the Spanish Netherlands (part of modern Belgium). At first the wind blew from the south-west, which helped the Spanish Armada on its way through the English Channel. This wind caused problems for the English ships and made it difficult for them to attack the Spanish ships. For ten days the English fleet of 80 ships with 9000 sailors chased the Spanish ships along the English Channel. The English fleet was commanded by Lord Howard of Effingham. His Vice Admiral was Sir Francis Drake.

The Spanish Armada anchored in formation near Calais. The English fleet sent in fireships in the middle of the night to break up the formation of the Spanish ships. The ships were made out of wood, and the Spaniards feared that their ships would catch fire. On sight of the fireships the Spanish ships fled in confusion. As they sailed northwards in the North Sea, running battles were fought between the Spanish and English ships. A great gale blew up and many Spanish ships were wrecked on the coasts of Scotland and Ireland. In September 1588, 69 ships from the Spanish Armada returned to Spain. Thus the Spanish had not been able to invade England. The English soldiers, who had been waiting at Tilbury near London under the command of the Earl of Leicester, were not needed. The Tudor government had also built a strong system of forts along the English coast, and set up early warning beacons (warning fires) along the south coast.

Why was the Spanish Armada defeated?

The Spaniards said that the Armada was defeated by the weather, particularly the great gale. The English said it was the skill of the English sailors and the skilled movements of their ships that had defeated the Armada. Queen Elizabeth I had a medal made. The words on it said 'God Blew and they were scattered'. The defeat of the Spanish Armada in 1588 lessened fears of a Catholic Spanish invasion. However, the war between England and Spain continued for a further 16 years.

Source C   Route of the Spanish Armada, 1588

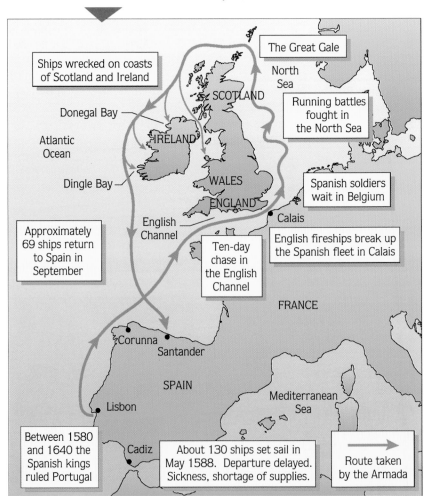

- The Great Gale
- Ships wrecked on coasts of Scotland and Ireland
- North Sea
- SCOTLAND
- Running battles fought in the North Sea
- Donegal Bay
- Atlantic Ocean
- IRELAND
- Dingle Bay
- WALES
- ENGLAND
- Spanish soldiers wait in Belgium
- Calais
- English Channel
- Approximately 69 ships return to Spain in September
- Ten-day chase in the English Channel
- English fireships break up the Spanish fleet in Calais
- FRANCE
- Corunna
- Santander
- SPAIN
- Mediterranean Sea
- Lisbon
- Between 1580 and 1640 the Spanish kings ruled Portugal
- Cadiz
- About 130 ships set sail in May 1588. Departure delayed. Sickness, shortage of supplies.
- Route taken by the Armada

Investigations

1 Using the information in the text, explain why England and Spain went to war.

2 Using the route map and the text, write about the difficulties met by the Spanish Armada from the time it left Spain. What part did English ships and sailors play in the defeat of the Armada?

Key words

Armada A fleet of ships.
Mercenary A soldier who fights for a foreign country for money.

Source D
Portrait of Queen Elizabeth I painted after the defeat of the Spanish Armada

Source E Medal made to celebrate victory over the Spanish Armada

3 Look at Source **D**.
a) Why was Elizabeth shown with two pictures (or windows) of the Armada in her portrait?
b) The picture is known as the 'Armada' portrait. Do you think that is a good title? Can you suggest another title?

4 The events on the map (Source **C**) tell the story of the Spanish Armada. Look at the sea route. Then rearrange the events listed below into chronological order:
• Fireships sent in and used near Calais;
• The great gale;
• Ships wrecked off Scotland and Ireland;
• Ten-day chase in the English Channel;
• Running battle in the North Sea.

5 The words on the medal (Source **E**) are 'God blew and they were scattered'. Who were 'they'?
a) The medal shows one explanation for the defeat of the Spanish Armada. What is it?
b) What connection can you see between the words written on the medal, and the pictures of the Armada in Source **D**?

23

Crown and Parliament

Today, the monarch in Britain has very little real power. Britain is governed by Parliament. There are two 'Houses' in Parliament. These are the **House of Commons** and the **House of Lords**. The government is made up of the party which has most members (MPs) in the House of Commons. The House of Commons and the House of Lords each meet separately without the monarch being present. However, on the occasion of the State Opening of Parliament the members of the two Houses meet together in the presence of the monarch.

In the sixteenth and seventeenth centuries there were no political parties like there are today, and there was no **Prime Minister** (pages 82–3). The monarch ruled the country. It was the monarch who decided when Parliament should meet together, or not meet. The most important power that Parliament had was that of voting for **taxes** to provide money for the monarch when it was needed. During the reign of Elizabeth I, Parliament became more powerful. In the late sixteenth century important changes took place in the balance of power between the monarchy, Parliament and people.

Source A Elizabeth I in Parliament (1584)

Key words

House of Commons The lower house of the British Parliament, made up of elected members.
House of Lords The upper house of the British Parliament, made up of lords and important Church leaders. Members of the House of Lords are not elected.
Prime Minister The most important minister of a monarch.
Taxes Money which people have to pay to the state.

Investigations

1 Compare Source **A** with Source **D** in Chapter 1 (page 9). How has the artist shown the monarch in a powerful position in both pictures?

2 The throne is placed on a carpet called the cloth of state. Henry VIII had an Act of Parliament passed which said that no one except the monarch was allowed on this carpet. How can you tell it was still the law in Elizabeth's reign?

3 In the picture made in 1523 (page 9), the abbots in charge of the monasteries are shown. Why are there no abbots in the picture of the Elizabethan Parliament (Chapter 4)?

The Stuarts and the Union of Crowns

Elizabeth I, the last of the Tudor monarchs, died without heirs in 1603. James Stuart, who as James VI was King of Scotland, was Elizabeth's closest living relative. He was the Protestant son of Mary Queen of Scots (pages 20–1) who had been executed by Elizabeth's government. He became King of England as James I. Thus the Crowns of Scotland and England became united under the Scottish house of Stuart.

Source A
The Coronation of James I in 1603

Investigations

1 Source **A** shows marked: (1) the queen, Anne of Denmark; (2, 3, 4) King James; (5, 6) two thrones; (7) the musicians; (8) the beacons to spread the news; (9) the ships in the river Thames firing canon salutes.
   a) What event is taking place in Westminster Abbey?
   b) How has the artist shown people celebrating the event?

2 Using the information in the picture and the number key write an account of the Coronation, beginning: 'We are at Westminster Abbey. The day is 25 July 1603 . . .' (now write on).

3 Look at the Coats of Arms on the left and right hand pillars. How has the artist shown that the Crowns of England and Scotland were now united?

4 Look at the lifeline of Mary Queen of Scots (page 21). How old was her son when the Crowns of Scotland and England were united in 1603?

5 What connections can you find between the coats of arms and emblems of James VI in Source **A** and those of James IV and Margaret shown in Source **F** of Chapter 1 (page 6). What relation was James VI to James IV?

3 Religious changes and conflict
The Reformation

- ***What did people believe before the Reformation?***
- ***When did the movement to reform the Church begin?***

For almost one thousand years, from the seventh century to the sixteenth century, Britain and other countries in Western Europe followed the same Christian religion. This was the Roman Catholic religion. The head of the Roman Catholic Church was the Pope in Rome. Some people in Europe followed other religions. These included the Jews and the Moslems. For almost everyone, whether Christian, Jew or Moslem, religion was a very important part of their everyday lives. This chapter is about the changes in religion which took place in many countries in Western Europe, and which greatly affected the lives of people in Britain.

In the later Middle Ages the people of Western Europe had suffered greatly from disease, famine and war. They began to think a lot about death and about sin. Many became afraid. They believed that God was punishing them for being wicked. Superstition was widespread. Some people began to complain about the Pope and about the great wealth of the Church. In England, John Wyclif (1324–84) said that the Church was too rich and powerful. Wyclif, and some other people, had ideas about improving the Church. However, no important changes took place at this time. It was not until the sixteenth century that important reform in religion took place.

Why did some people in the sixteenth century want reform of the Church?

By the early sixteenth century more and more people began to speak out against the Church. They were sometimes shocked by the behaviour of the Pope and some of the Church leaders. In some parishes the clergy were not doing their work properly, or looking after the needs of the people. About this time a Dutch scholar, called Erasmus (1469–1536), travelled to many parts of Europe to talk about his ideas of reforming the Church. He wanted to make the ways of the Church easier for ordinary people to understand. He wanted simple everyday words used at Church services instead of the Latin language. More and more people began to support the idea that the Church needed to be reformed. However, the Pope and important people in the Church, were against change. They tried to stop the idea of reform from spreading.

When and why did the Protestant Reformation begin?

The Pope tried to raise money for the building of St. Peter's Church in Rome by selling **indulgences** in many parts of Europe. In Germany, in 1517, a Catholic monk called Martin Luther protested against this. The protest against the selling of indulgences led to people attacking many of the ways of the Church. The Pope **excommunicated** Luther. This meant that Luther was no longer a member of the Catholic Church. Luther publicly burned the Pope's letter (known as a **papal bull**) and set out his own ideas for the reform of the Church.

Source A

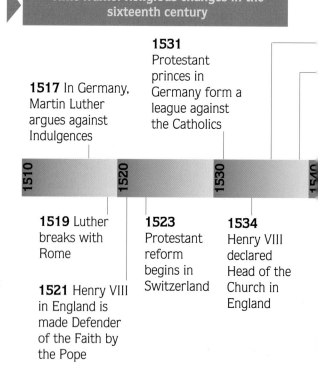

Time frame: Religious changes in the sixteenth century

1517 In Germany, Martin Luther argues against Indulgences

1519 Luther breaks with Rome

1521 Henry VIII in England is made Defender of the Faith by the Pope

1523 Protestant reform begins in Switzerland

1531 Protestant princes in Germany form a league against the Catholics

1534 Henry VIII declared Head of the Church in England

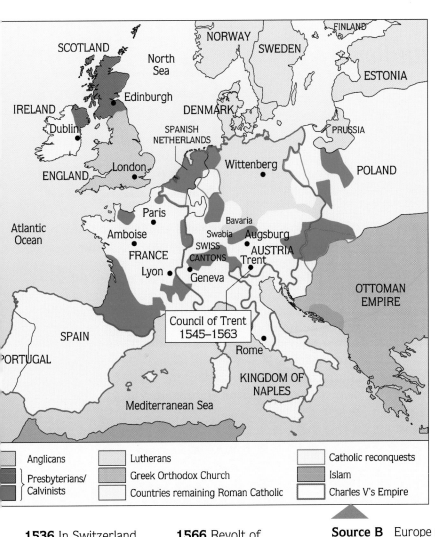

How were religion and politics linked?

In the sixteenth century there were close links between religion and politics. The rulers of some European countries supported the ideas of Martin Luther. They wanted the **Reformation** of the Church. Other rulers continued to support the old Roman Catholic religion and the Pope. These differences between rulers, peoples and countries soon led to arguments and to religious wars. Gradually, much of northern Germany, Switzerland, Holland, Scandinavia, England and Scotland became Protestant. Other parts of Europe, southern Germany, the Italian states, France, Spain and Portugal remained Roman Catholic. Sometimes however, within each country, each town and even within the same families there were Catholics and Protestants. Sometimes they did not agree. These disagreements caused wars in many parts of Europe.

Map key:

Anglicans	Lutherans
Presbyterians/Calvinists	Greek Orthodox Church
	Countries remaining Roman Catholic
Catholic reconquests	Islam
Charles V's Empire	

Source B Europe after the Reformation

1536 In Switzerland, John Calvin publishes his ideas for Protestant reform

1539 English translation of the Bible.

1545 Meeting of Council of Trent in Germany – the Counter-Reformation

1556 Archbishop Thomas Cranmer burned at the stake in England

1559 John Knox brings Protestant ideas of Calvin to Scotland

1566 Revolt of Protestant Netherlands against Catholic Spain

1570 The Pope in Rome excommunicates Queen Elizabeth in England

1572 Massacre of St Bartholomew in France – many Huguenot Protestants killed

1588 Welsh translation of the Bible

1605 Gunpowder Plot in England

1611 King James orders new version of the Bible in English

1620 The Pilgrim Fathers settle in New England (America)

Timeline: 1550, 1560, 1570, 1580, 1590, 1600, 1610, 1620

Key words

Indulgences Letting sinners off the punishment they would receive for their sins after death.
Excommunicated Expelled from the Church.
Papal bull Command, letter or order from the Pope.
Reformation The movement for the reform of the Catholic Church.

Investigations

1 Using the information in the text and the time frame (Source **A**) would you say the changes took place slowly or quickly?

2 Using Sources **A** and **B** say how the religious changes affected most countries in Europe. How do the sources show that there were also changes and religious differences within countries?

3 Explain how the changes in religion which led to differences between and within countries might lead to wars.

England's break with Rome

Why did Henry VIII quarrel with the Pope?

Source A Extract from The Act of Supremacy (1534)

The king ... his heirs and successors ... shall be ... accepted (as) ... the only supreme head in earth of the Church in England ...

In 1521 Henry VIII wrote a book defending the Catholic Church against the attacks of Luther and the Reformers. The Pope awarded Henry the title Defender of the Faith (in Latin *Fidei Defensor*). The letters FD which stand for this title can still be seen on our coins today. Henry was a religious man and a firm believer in the Catholic Church. However, there was one matter on which the king and the Pope could not agree.

Henry VIII and his first wife Catherine of Aragon had only one child, a daughter called Mary. England had never been ruled by a queen and Henry wanted a son who could become king after him. At this time England was a Roman Catholic country and the Pope in Rome was the head of the Church. Henry's chief minister was Thomas Wolsey. As well as being the king's minister, Wolsey was also a Cardinal in the Roman Catholic Church. Henry wanted a divorce so that he could marry again. He asked Wolsey to get the Pope to agree to it. When the Pope refused the request, Henry **dismissed** Wolsey (page 9).

The break from Rome

Henry decided to break away from Rome. On the advice of Thomas Cranmer, the Archbishop of Canterbury, Henry announced himself divorced. He said that he would stop paying taxes to the Church. At the same time, some people did not like the fact that the Pope in Rome was head of the Catholic Church in England. They said that the Church was too rich and powerful. They said that some priests did not act in a Christian way. In general, people who lived in the countryside were more likely to support the old ways and stay faithful to the Catholic Church.

People who lived in towns and in cities like London were more likely to support the idea of change.

The English Parliament played an important part in the break from Rome by passing a number of Acts. In 1534 Parliament passed a law called the Act of Supremacy. This said that Henry VIII was the **supreme head** on earth of the Church in England. At the time of the break with Rome, Thomas Cromwell was Henry's chief adviser. He was also in charge of state affairs during the time of Henry's divorce from Catherine and his marriage to Anne Boleyn.

Source B The king replaces the Pope as head of the Church in England

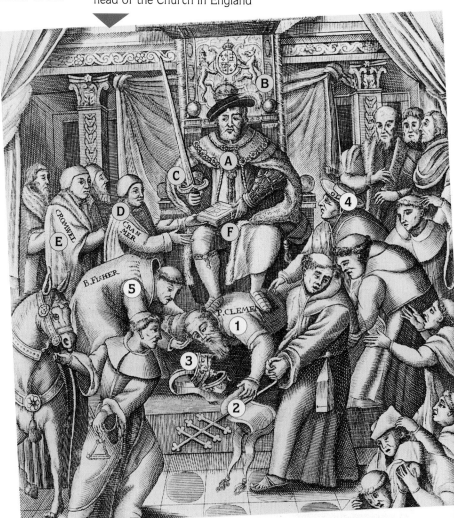

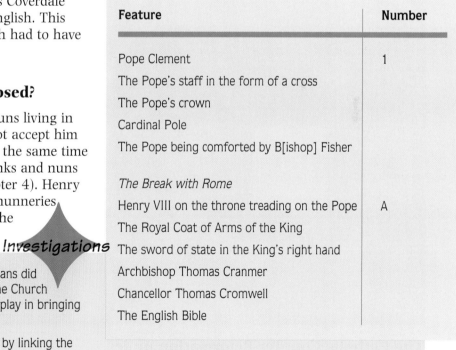

When did the Reformation begin in England?

The Protestant Reformation in England began with Henry VIII's break from Rome over his divorce from Catherine of Aragon. However, Henry himself stayed true to many of the old Catholic beliefs. With the Archbishop of Canterbury, Thomas Cranmer, Henry tried to get agreement between the old (Catholic) and new (Protestant) religious beliefs. Some people did not agree with the Act of Supremacy and this made Henry angry. Sir Thomas More, who had been a good friend of the king, and his chief minister, refused to accept that Henry was the Head of the Church in England. Sir Thomas More was imprisoned, and later executed. Henry would not stand for anyone opposing him on matters of religion, whether Catholic or Protestant.

There were also other changes. The Protestant Reformers, William Tyndale and Miles Coverdale translated the Bible from Latin into English. This was printed in 1539 and every church had to have one.

Why were the Monasteries closed?

Henry feared that some monks and nuns living in monasteries and **nunneries** might not accept him as Head of the Church in England. At the same time some people were saying that the monks and nuns were becoming lazy and greedy (Chapter 4). Henry decided to close the monasteries and nunneries. This is known as the **dissolution** of the

monasteries. The lands which belonged to them became the property of the Crown. Much of this land was later sold or given to the nobility and the gentry. In this way, money was raised for the Crown (page 44).

Feature	Number
Pope Clement	1
The Pope's staff in the form of a cross	
The Pope's crown	
Cardinal Pole	
The Pope being comforted by B[ishop] Fisher	
The Break with Rome	
Henry VIII on the throne treading on the Pope	A
The Royal Coat of Arms of the King	
The sword of state in the King's right hand	
Archbishop Thomas Cranmer	
Chancellor Thomas Cromwell	
The English Bible	

Investigations

1 Read Source **A**. When and by what means did Henry VIII become supreme head of the Church in England? What part did Parliament play in bringing about religious change?

2 Identify the main features in Source **B** by linking the numbers and letters in the picture with the correct descriptions in the chart on the right. The first number and letter have been done for you.

3 How did the break with Rome increase the power and responsibilities of the King of England?

Key words

Dismissed   Sent away or losing a job or position.
Supreme head   The highest in rank.
Nunneries   Places where groups of nuns (holy women) lived a religious life.

Dissolution   To bring to an end, for example the closure of the monasteries.

Depth Study:
The Reformation and Counter-Reformation

When did England become a Protestant country?

During the short reign of the boy king, Edward VI (1547–53), the Crown and Parliament continued to take church property by passing further Acts. Any remaining monasteries were closed. There was also an attempt to reform some of the religious ways of the time. The **ministers** of the king, particularly the Archbishop of Canterbury, Thomas Cranmer, wanted to bring in Protestant ways of worship. Many of the old Catholic statues and paintings were destroyed. A new prayer book was introduced and church services were made more simple.

Source A The Reformation continues under King Edward VI

The Catholic Counter-Reformation under Mary I

During Mary I's short reign (1553–8) attempts were made to bring back the Roman Catholic religion in England. This is known as a Counter-Reformation. Mary had followed the Roman Catholic faith all her life. As queen, she tried to reverse (or counter) the religious changes that had been made in the reigns of Henry VIII and Edward VI. Her loyalty to Catholicism led to about 300 Protestants being burned at the stake. Included amongst these was the Archbishop of Canterbury, Thomas Cranmer, who was executed for high treason. Those who spoke out against Catholic beliefs might be persecuted.

Source B The last moments of Archbishop Thomas Cranmer (from John Foxe's *Book of Martyrs*)

The burnyng of the Archbishop of Caunterbury Doctor Thomas Cranmer, in the Towneditch at Oxforde, with his hand first thrust into the fire, wherewith he subscribed before.

Lord receiue my spirit

Source C From the Spanish Ambassador in London writing in 1555 to King Philip of Spain about the burning of a Protestant at the stake

A certain Rogers was burned publicly yesterday. Some of the onlookers wept, others prayed to God to give him strength to bear the pain, others gathered the ashes and the bones and wrapped them in paper to preserve them ... I think it would be wise not to be too firm against Protestants, otherwise I foresee that the people may cause a revolt. The lady Elizabeth has her supporters, and there are Englishmen who do not love foreigners.

Investigations

1 Identify the main features in Source **A** by linking the numbers in the picture with the correct descriptions in the chart below. The first one is done for you.

Feature	Number
King Henry VIII on his death bed	1
The boy king, Edward VI on a small throne	
The Royal Arms above the throne	
The new English prayer book which strikes the Pope's head	
The Pope with his staff	
The Protestant Protector, the Duke of Somerset seen standing	
The Archbishop of Canterbury, Thomas Cranmer	
King Edward's Council of advisers around the table	

2 Which two features in the painting show that Henry VIII intended his son to be the next king?

3 How does the picture show that the new English prayer book of 1549 was a 'blow' to the Pope in Rome. Can you explain why?

4 Through the window (Source **A**) Catholic statues are being destroyed. How is this showing that the Refomation continued during the reign of Edward VI?

5 What events are taking place in Sources **B** and **C**? During whose reign did these events take place?

6 Which Archbishop can be seen in Source **B**? Of what was he accused and found guilty? Where did his execution take place?

7 Source **B** is from a *Book of Martyrs* by a Protestant named John Foxe. It showed Protestants being tortured, burned and executed. How might this popular book, published after Mary's death, help give her the nickname 'Bloody Mary'? How might the book and its pictures be one-sided (biased)?

8 Why was the Catholic Spanish Ambassador (Source **C**) concerned about the execution of Protestants in England?

Key words

Ministers People who have important positions in government.

How did Elizabeth I try to settle the religious differences?

When Mary died in 1558, her half-sister, Elizabeth, became Queen. At this time there were many quarrels over religion between Catholics and Protestants. Elizabeth and her ministers wanted to settle some of the quarrels. The Protestant Settlement of 1563 returned the country back to Protestantism and made the Church of England the **established Church** of the country. A new prayer book and the Thirty Nine Articles (rules) set out the main beliefs of this established Church. For the first years of Elizabeth's reign the Protestant Settlement worked well and was accepted by most people.

How did Protestantism affect Wales?

As England became Protestant, so too did Wales. A new Welsh prayer book was published in 1567. Even more important was the translation of the Bible into Welsh in 1588. This was largely the work of William Morgan. These books helped to keep the Welsh language alive and enabled the people in Wales to keep something of their own culture.

Source E   The Bible in Welsh 1588

Why did religious persecution increase in the last years of Elizabeth's reign?

In 1569 some Catholic nobles in the north of England rose up in **revolt** against Elizabeth. This Rising of the Northern Earls, as it became known, was defeated. In the following year, 1570, the Pope in Rome excommunicated Elizabeth. Elizabeth began to treat Roman Catholics more harshly. Many of the ways of the Catholic religion were forbidden. These included Catholic books, the ringing of bells to call for prayers for the dead, the use of **rosary beads**, making the sign of the cross and keeping Catholic feast days.

Catholic priests, trained at Douay in France, came to England secretly to serve the remaining Catholics, known as **recusants**. To avoid being discovered a Catholic priest might have to hide in places called priests' holes. These were secret places built in the houses of some of those nobles who had stayed Catholic. Many Catholics were tortured and put to death for giving priests a place to hide. One such person was Margaret Clitherow of York, the wife of a wealthy butcher.

A few Catholics plotted to remove Elizabeth as queen and put her cousin Mary Queen of Scots on the throne instead (pages 20–1). In the later years of Elizabeth's reign, the persecution of Catholics increased. Parliament passed an Act in 1585 which said that Roman Catholic priests could be put to death if caught.

Source G Two Catholic priests sent to England

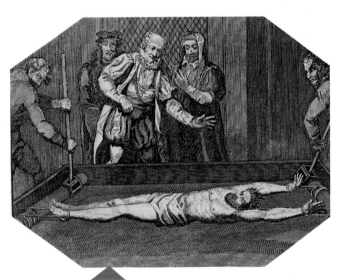

Y ou must return (to prison) ... and there ... be stripped naked, laid on your back next to the ground, and as much weight laid upon you as you are able to bear, and so continue three days without any food except a little barley bread and puddle water, and the third day to be pressed to death, your hands and feet tied to posts, and a sharp stone under your back.

Source H An English Catholic on the rack

Source I A judge in York orders the punishment of Margaret Clitherow

Investigations

1 What books do Sources **D** and **E** show? In which two languages are they written?

2 Give two reasons why the printed Bibles in English and Welsh would be read by more people than the hand-written Latin Bible of earlier times?

3 How might a Bible written in Welsh help to keep alive the language and culture of Wales?

4 Look at Source **F**.
a) What did the Pope write out and sign to show that Elizabeth was excommunicated?
b) How was the Papal Bull sent to Elizabeth in England?
c) Why might Catholics in England fear the consequences of Elizabeth being excommunicated?

5 Source **G** shows two Catholic priests who came to England in 1580. Why did they come in secret? Why and how might some Catholic families hide priests?

6 How do the sources show that Catholics were tortured and persecuted during the reign of Elizabeth I?

7 Margaret Clitherow was arrested in 1586 for hiding priests. She refused to say whether she was guilty or not guilty. Why do you think she was punished by a long, slow death (Source **I**)?

8 Why would you not want to be a Protestant in the reign of Mary I, or a Catholic in the reign of Elizabeth 1?

Key words

Established Church The Church of England as set up (that is, established) by Acts of Parliament.
Revolt A rebellion against those in authority.
Rosary beads A string of beads used for praying in the Roman Catholic Church.
Recusants People who refused to attend Church of England services.

The Reformation in Scotland

In the sixteenth century, many people in Scotland also wanted changes in religion. The Scottish reformers learned about Protestantism from a man called John Knox. Knox had worked in Geneva (in Switzerland) with a Protestant reformer called John Calvin. When Knox returned to Scotland in 1559 he brought the new Protestant ideas with him. He became a leader of a group who were against Mary Stuart, the Catholic Queen of Scotland. The Protestant Church in Scotland is known as the Presbyterian Church. Its rules were set out in the *Scots Confession* and the *Book of Common Order*. The Church of Scotland became the most important Presbyterian Church in Britain.

The Puritans

From the time of Elizabeth I, some Protestants were dissatisfied with the Church of England and wanted to reform it. These reformers were called Puritans. When Elizabeth I died in 1603, James I (James VI of Scotland) became king. He reigned from 1603 to 1625. He was not a popular king. During his reign people were fined if they did not attend Church of England services. The Puritans were disappointed that James I did not make the Church of England more like the Scottish Presbyterian Church. Catholics were also against James I's strict religious rules. The king had reason, therefore, to fear both the Puritans and the Catholics.

The Pilgrim Fathers

During the reign of James I, the Puritans became more critical of the Church of England. To escape persecution, some Puritans left England to settle in Holland. In 1620 about 100 English Puritans, who had lived in **exile** in Holland for some years, set sail for America in a ship called *Mayflower*. They landed at Plymouth, Massachusetts on the east coast of America and settled there.

The Ulster Plantation

In the long term, the Protestant Reformation made relations between England and Ireland worse. England became mainly a Protestant country but most people in Ireland stayed Catholic. By the end of Elizabeth's reign, a serious rebellion in Ireland had been defeated. During the reign of James I, Scottish and English Protestants were allowed to settle in the north of Ireland (Ulster). The native Irish

Source J Picture from the *First Blast of the Trumpet Against the Monstrous Regiment of Women*, by John Knox

Source K Extract from *First Blast ...*, by John Knox

> To promote a woman to ... rule ... any ... nation ... is repugnant (offensive) to nature ... to God ... good order ... and justice.

people were removed from their land by force. This was to clear the way for the new Protestant settlers. By 1640 more than 30,000 Scottish and English Protestants had settled in Ireland. Towns such as Londonderry and Belfast were developed.

Investigations

1 Look at Sources **J** and **K**. Did John Knox think well of women or not? What evidence in the sources supports your answer? Might men living in the sixteenth century have agreed with the views of Knox?

2 John Knox described women as 'frail, weak, feeble and impatient creatures'. Do you think this description 'fitted' Mary Queen of Scots or Queen Elizabeth I?

3 Using Sources **J** and **K**, and the text, can you say why arguments might occur between Knox (spelt Knokes in Source **J**) and Mary Queen of Scots? Why were they enemies?

4 Why did Knox encourage the destruction of statues and pictures in Catholic Churches?

5 In what ways were the religious changes in Scotland different to those in England?

Key words

Exile Choosing, or being made, to live in another country.

34

An Age of Witchcraft

For many centuries, the people of Western Europe were very superstitious. Witchcraft is one kind of supersitition. In the sixteenth and seventeenth centuries, over 100,000 people throughout Europe were accused of witchcraft and put to death. Fear of witchcraft grew after the Reformation. In many Protestant countries, people could no longer turn to religious practices such as **holy water**, **processions** and **saints days** to protect them against misfortune. As they looked for someone or something to blame, accusations and prosecutions of so-called witches increased.

Most people accused of witchcraft were women, usually widows or unmarried women who lived on their own. Often they were poor or elderly. They were usually people who did not mix much in the local community. They were therefore an easy target when people were looking for someone to blame for a misfortune.

Witches were accused of such tricks as turning milk sour and causing storms. They were often blamed for local misfortunes such as ruined crops, injury or the death of animals or people, outbreaks of disease, accidents and quarrels between neighbours.

executed for witchcraft, mostly during the reigns of Elizabeth I and James I. In the 1590s there were witch hunts in Scotland. Torture was often used to make witches confess and to get them to 'name' other witches. By the eighteenth century, belief in witches and witchcraft was declining, although it still existed in some country areas.

How were witches treated?

In 1542 witchcraft became punishable by death. For almost 150 years, until 1685 when the last trial was held for witchcraft, thousands of people, almost all of them women, were accused of being witches. In England over 1000 people were

Key words

Holy water Water blessed by a priest and used in religious services.
Processions People moving forward in an orderly way, for example at a festival, a religious celebration.
Saints days Days of Church festivals and services in memory of saints.

Investigations

1 Explain what is happening in Source **A** by answering the following questions:
   a) Who is being held by a rope in the water?
   b) Why did some people blame witches for their misfortunes?

2 What 'misfortunes' can be seen in the picture? For example:
   a) What has happened to the cart?
   b) Why are the piglets in the water?
   c) Why is the man on the roof of the water-mill?

3 How many magistrates are watching the 'swimming of the suspected witch'?

The Gunpowder Plot

What did the government know and when?

A number of Catholics led by a man called Robert Catesby planned to blow up the king and Parliament. They chose 5 November 1605, the date of the State Opening of Parliament. This was the time when the king, his ministers and all the members of Parliament would be present. The chief minister of the king, Robert Cecil, found out about the plot. However, he did nothing about it at first. Then, on the night before the State Opening, he had the cellars under Parliament searched. Guy Fawkes, one of the plotters, was found there, together with barrels of gunpowder and a tinderbox. Two of the plotters, Guy Fawkes and Robert Winter, were arrested. They were tortured until they **confessed**. The remaining plotters, who had fled to other parts of the country, were hunted down. Four of them were shot. At the trial of Guy Fawkes and his fellow **conspirators**, the only evidence used to prove their guilt were the confessions which had been made by Fawkes and Winter under torture. The plotters were found guilty and put to death. The Gunpowder Plot is remembered on November 5th each year as 'bonfire night'.

Source B   The signature of Guy Fawkes before and after he was 'questioned'

Source C   Execution of one of the Gunpowder plotters

Investigations

1 The artist who drew Source **A** has given the names of the gunpowder plotters. What are they?

2 Why did the plotters choose 5 November 1605 to carry out their plan?

3 Source **B** shows the signature of Guy Fawkes before and after he was arrested. In what ways are they different?
   a) What may have caused the change in his handwriting, and also have caused Fawkes to confess to the Gunpowder Plot?
   b) Do you think the confessions of Fawkes and Winter under torture proved they were guilty?

4 How might the attempt to blow up Parliament make the king and his government more popular?

Key words

Confessed   Admitted to doing something.
Conspirators   People who secretly plot to do harm, usually for political reasons.

How did King James I try to unite the country in religion?

Religion can sometimes be important in uniting families, communities and countries. Monarchs often recognised the importance of **religious unity** in holding a country together. However, the religious changes of the Reformation had led to **disunity** both within and between countries. The Gunpowder Plot of the Catholics, and the opposition of the Puritans convinced James I of the need for greater unity. For this reason the king encouraged the Church of England bishops to use the Church courts to remove the more extreme ways of worship. In addition, a new version of the English Bible was published in 1611. It is known as the **Authorised** (King James)

Source D Cartoon called *The Double Deliverance*

Bible. However, neither the King nor the Church of England were able to re-unite the country in religion.

Investigations

5 Identify the main features in the cartoon (Source **D**) by linking the numbers and letters in the picture with the correct descriptions in the chart on the right. The first number and letter is done for you.

6 The cartoon shows two events that threatened England. What are they? Which event came first in time, and which came second? Who is shown 'delivering' England from the two threats?

7 In what ways do you think the cartoon is giving a one-sided (biased) view?

8 How many years had passed between the first English translation of the Bible (pages 26–7) and the Bible of 1611?

Feature	Number
The Pope with his staff	1
The King of Spain	
The Spanish Armada of ships	
Guy Fawkes with his lantern	
Barrels of Gunpowder in the cellars of the Houses of Parliament	
God in Heaven shown protecting England	A
The wind blowing to scatter the Armada	
The eye of God seeing the Gunpowder Plot	

Key words

Religious unity Being one in religion. Cooperation and harmony between different religions.
Disunity Being divided

Authorised To give permission or authority for something to be done.

4 Dissolution of the Monasteries

The monasteries before the Dissolution

Henry VIII broke away from the Pope in Rome. He became head of the Church in England by an Act of Parliament called the Act of Supremacy. Some people did not accept Henry as Head of the Church in England. Included amongst these were some monks and nuns who Henry feared might be against him. Henry's chief adviser at this time was a man called Thomas Cromwell. Cromwell sent men to visit the **religious houses** (monasteries and nunneries) where the monks and nuns lived. These men were called commissioners or inspectors. Their job was to find out about the wealth and the property owned by the religious houses. Some people felt that, although many monks and nuns did good work, a few had become lazy and greedy. This gave Henry an excuse to dissolve (that is to close down) those religious houses that the royal inspectors said were unfit. Most of the monasteries and nunneries were dissolved between 1536 and 1540. The property and land belonging to them went to the Crown. Henry kept the riches for himself and sold much of the land.

Source A Castle Acre Priory in Norfolk before the Dissolution

Source B Castle Acre Priory in Norfolk after the Dissolution

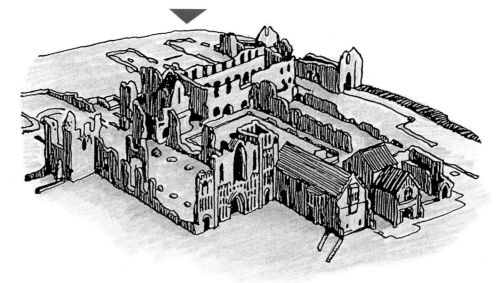

1485? Born, the son of a blacksmith, brewer and innkeeper

1504? Went to Italy, possibly as a mercenary soldier fighting for France

1513 Wool trader, money lender and law business

1533 Appointed Chancellor

1534 Became Secretary of Henry VIII

1536–9 Carried out dissolution of the monasteries. Acquired property from this

1540 Accused of high treason and executed

| 1480 | 1490 | 1500 | 1510 | 1520 | 1530 | 1540 |

1512 Merchant at Antwerp and Middelburg
c.1512 Returned to England and married Elizabeth Wykes

1523 Elected as a member of Parliament

1531 Became a member of Henry VIII's Council

1539–40 Arranged Henry VIII's unsuccessful marriage to Anne of Cleves

1514 Collector of money for Archbishop of York, Thomas Wolsey

Source C Portrait of Thomas Cromwell

EARL OF ESSEX.

Investigations

1 What differences can you see between Sources **A** and **B**?

2 Using Sources **A** and **B** and the information below, write out six questions each beginning with a key word: who, why, how, where, when, what. In pairs or groups, compare your questions and decide which are the most important.
   • England and Wales:
   • Before 1536 – 800 monasteries and nunneries; 10, 000 monks and nuns.
   • After 1540 – no monasteries and nunneries.

3 How does Thomas Cromwell's lifeline show that not much is known about his early life?

4 Why did Henry VIII and Thomas Cromwell want to close down the monasteries?

5 The commissioners (inspectors) visited the monasteries and convents with a list of questions. What questions do you think they asked?

6 Do you think the commissioners were looking for good things or bad things when they inspected the monasteries and nunneries? Can you explain your answer?

Key words

Religious houses Often described simply as monasteries, religious houses included abbeys, convents, friaries, hospices, nunneries and priories.

Source D An Inspector visits a monastery

The visitors ... entered ... the gates, they called the abbot and other officers of the house and caused them to deliver all the keys, and took an inventory of all their goods, both within doors and without. For all such beasts, horses, sheep and such cattle as were abroad in pasture or grange (farm) places, the visitors caused to be brought into their presence ...

From a manuscript in the British Museum quoted in Michael Roulstone *The Royal House of Tudor*, Balfour Publications, 1974

Source E Trying to keep the secrets of a convent – St Edmund's convent in Suffolk

I could not find out anything bad about the convent, no matter how hard I tried. I believe I couldn't find anything because everybody had got together and agreed to keep the convent's secrets.

Sources F to J: short extracts from Commissioners' Reports to Thomas Cromwell

Source F Woolsthorpe in Lincolnshire

The governor (abbot) ... is well beloved, having eight ... priests ... living religiously ... embroidering, writing books ... making their own garments, carving, painting or engraving ...

Source G St Edmund's monastery in Suffolk

The Abbot delighted much in playing at dice and in that spent much money. For his own pleasure he has had lots of beautiful buildings built ...

Source H Ramsey priory

Many of the monks devote themselves more to hunting and other sports ... sometimes some of them shoot arrows in the fields in unbecoming attire. The dormitory is in ... disrepair ... rain falls on the beds ... The prior ... is frequently drunk.

Source I Peterborough monastery

The ... abbot does not choose studious monks but looks for lazy ones. Within the monastery there is a ... tavern in which the brethren (monks) drink ... The ... abbot sells cattle of (belonging to) the monastery, and keeps the money for himself.

Source J Pentney priory in Norfolk

A house that feeds so many poor ... is in a good state, maintains good service, and does so many charitable (good) deeds.

Investigations

7 Using the information in Sources **F** to **J**, list the good things and the bad things that the commissioners found in the five religious houses.

8 Given the good and bad reports on the monasteries do you think that:

a) the monasteries should be closed down,
b) the monasteries should stay as they are, or
c) some other action should be taken?

9 Why might some people miss the monasteries if they were closed down?

The Pilgrimage of Grace

Why did some people join the Pilgrimage of Grace?

In 1536–7 there was a great northern uprising. The rebels were against the changes brought about by the king and his advisers, especially Thomas Cromwell. The uprising became known as the Pilgrimage of Grace. It began in Lincolnshire and Yorkshire and was led by Robert Aske. There were a number of reasons for the Pilgrimage of Grace. One of the most important reasons was dislike of the religious changes of the 1530s, particularly the dissolution of the monasteries. The results of the enclosure of farm land (page 91) were also reasons for the uprising. At one point, the rebels were in control of York, the most important city in northern England. A **truce** was called. The rebels thought they had got what they wanted and they promised to be loyal to the king. However, their demands were not met, and a further revolt took place in 1537. The uprising was eventually defeated and over 200 of the rebels were executed.

Source A The Pilgrimage of Grace

Key words

Truce An agreement for ending, usually for a short period of time, armed hostilities.

Source B

Reasons for joining the Pilgrimage of Grace
1 To give back some powers to the Pope in Rome
2 To give the monasteries which had been closed back to the monks
3 To punish Thomas Cromwell, and members of the King's Council
4 To stop the enclosure of farmland
5 To be free of the new taxes passed by Parliament
6 To have a Parliament in the north of England to talk about people's grievances
7 Food shortages, bad weather and poor harvests
8 To make Princess Mary legitimate and heir to the throne
9 To make sure the Catholic Church survived in England

Investigations

1 Explain what you can see in Source **A**. Does it show:
   a) pilgrims on their way to a holy place
   b) rebels protesting against the changes made by the king and his advisers
   c) courtiers leading a procession in praise of the king?

2 People joined the Pilgrimage of Grace for many reasons. These included religious, political and economic reasons. Look at the reasons in the box above. Then make a copy of the table on the right and place the correct numbers in the spaces.

Religious reasons for joining the Pilgrimage	Political reasons for joining the Pilgrimage	Economic reasons for for joining the Pilgrimage
Numbers	Numbers	Numbers

List your reasons in order of importance.

Source C The Pilgrims' Oath

Enter this our Pilgrimage of Grace ... only for the love that ye do bear unto Almighty God ... and the Holy Church ... to the preservation of the ... King's person and his issue ... and to expulse all ... evil councillors ... from ... his Council ... enter into ... our Pilgrimage for no ... profit to yourself .... and take afore you the Cross of Christ, and in your hearts His Faith ...

Source D A ballad (or marching song) of the Pilgrims

Alack! Alack!
For the Churches Sake
Poor commons wake
And no man marvel
For clear it is
The decay of this
How the poor shall miss
No tongue can tell

For there they had
Both ale and bread
In time of need
and succour great
In all distress
and Heaviness
And well intreat

Source E The badge of the rebels (showing the five wounds of Jesus)

Source F Syon convent or nunnery being closed by royal officials

Source G The Abbot of Colchester resists Dissolution of his Abbey

The King shall never have my house but against my will and against my heart, for I know by my learning that he cannot take it by right and law.

Source H The scene at Colchester after the dissolution of the Abbey

Investigations

3 How might Sources **C**, **D** and **E** help the 'pilgrims' to feel united?

4 Robert Aske wrote the oath (Source **C**) which the Pilgrims took in 1536. What does it tell you about the aims of the Pilgrims ? Did they blame the king or did they blame his advisers?

5 Can you explain why some people called the events of 1536–7 a Pilgrimage, while others called it a rebellion?

6 How can you tell that Source **F** shows a scene inside a nunnery?

7 What is taking place? Whose property is being removed, and why? Are the nuns accepting, or protesting against, the activities of the royal officials?

8 The picture was painted in the nineteenth century, three hundred years after the event shown. Is the artist on the side of the nuns or the royal officials? Explain your answer.

9 Why do you think the Abbot of Colchester was executed?

10 Identify the main features in Source **H** by linking the numbers in the picture with the descriptions in the chart below. The first one is done for you:

Feature	Number
A herald blowing a horn to announce the procession	1
The judge (who had sentenced the Abbot to death) on his horse with his staff of office	
A soldier escorting the procession	
The hill on which the execution of the Abbot took place	
A man kneeling as the judge passes	

The Chantries Act

During the reign of Edward VI nearly all the remaining monasteries and religious houses were dissolved. In 1547, an Act of Parliament was passed called the **Chantries** Act. Under this Act, many important churches became ordinary parish churches. Their lands and property were taken by the Crown. Also during Edward's reign much of the silver and gold altar plate, vestments (religious clothing) and other valuables belonging to the churches were taken by the Crown. In the late 1540s many religious gilds (societies) and religious shrines (holy places) were closed down. Some of the money was used to set up new schools. These were known as King Edward Grammar Schools.

The consequences of the Dissolution

Taking the property, lands and riches belonging to the monasteries made the Crown more wealthy. However, the closure of the monasteries meant that poor and sick people no longer had the monks and nuns to help them. Travellers could no longer stay at the monasteries on their journeys. As the buildings fell into ruin, new owners of the land which had once belonged to the monasteries often built themselves large houses with the stone.

Source I Buckland Abbey, the home of Sir Francis Drake after 1581

Investigations

1 The following information is not in correct order of time. Match the dates and events, and write them out correctly to show the history of Buckland Abbey.

Date	Event
13th century	Abbey bought by Sir Francis Drake
1536–9	Built by the Cistercian monks
1570s	Museum of the National Trust
1581	Becomes a country house
1996	Dissolution of the monasteries

2 What happened to much of the land taken from the monasteries?

3 Buckland Abbey was bought by Sir Francis Drake in 1581. How had Drake gained much money and wealth in the years 1577–80 (page 18)?

4 How can you tell that the building shown in Source I was once an abbey? What event first led to its change of use?

5 Most of the monasteries which were dissolved in the Tudor period are now in ruins. Do you think they should be preserved?

Key words

Chantries Chapels set up by individuals who, when they died, left money for religious services in their memory.

44

5 The Civil Wars

Crown and Parliament under the early Stuart kings

Why was there a struggle for power between the Crown and Parliament?

By the early seventeenth century, many economic, social and religious changes had taken place in the country. This led many people to question whether the monarch and the Church of England had too much power. The people who were questioning the power of the monarch included **Members of Parliament**. They wanted more influence over the way the country was governed. On the other hand, many European monarchs, including the Stuart kings in Britain (that is James I and later his son Charles I) believed in the **Divine Right of Kings**. This means that they believed that God had given them the right to rule. These different points of view led to political and religious problems and to arguments between the Crown, Parliament and the people in the mid-seventeenth century.

Source A
The House of Commons in the seventeenth century (c.1624)

Key words

Members of Parliament People elected as representatives in Parliament. Until the twentieth century there were no women members of Parliament.
Divine Right of Kings The belief that monarchs reign over their countries with the blessing and permission of the Christian God. Kings do not have to obey any earthly power, only God.

Investigations

1 Source **A** shows the House of Commons. What was the building used for?

2 Identify the main features in Source **A** by linking the numbers in the picture with the correct descriptions in the chart on the right. The first one is done for you.

3 Which person has the most important position in the scene of the House of Commons?

4 What are the main differences between the House of Commons (as shown in Source **A**) and the House of Lords (as shown in Source **A**, page 24)?

5 How do such sources help in understanding the work of Parliament?

Feature	Number
The Speaker	1
The members of the House of Commons	
Holder of the mace, symbol of the rights and privileges of the House	
The clerks at their table recording the meeting	
The Speaker's chair	

Why did James I argue with Parliament?

James I did not get on well with Parliament. This was partly due to the King's belief that God had given him the right to rule. James was also unpopular because he was too much influenced by his friends and favourites at the royal court. Towards the end of James I's reign his son, Charles, and a courtier called the Duke of Buckingham, took much of the power of the Crown upon themselves.

Source B

The Divine Right of Kings and the growing power of Parliament

The King is ... father of his people... it is wrong for subjects to argue about what a King may do...
I will not be happy that my power be questioned ...
1610

The freedoms of Parliament are the right of the people of England ... the keeping and making of laws are proper ... for Parliament.
In the handling of business every ... member of the House of Commons has ... freedom of speech ...
1621

Why did quarrels occur between Charles I and Parliament?

When James I died in 1625, his son Charles (1625–49) became king. Like his father before him, Charles quarrelled with Parliament. Sometimes quarrels took place because of the personalities of the people concerned. For example, although Charles I was a sincere person and was kind to his family, he did not understand what life was like for many of his **subjects**. Charles also believed that God had given him the right to rule. The way Charles and his ministers ruled the country caused ill-feeling and disagreements between the Crown and Parliament. Charles strongly supported the Church of England. His religious beliefs were very different to those of the Puritans (page 34), especially the growing number of Puritans in Parliament. The marriage of Charles I to the French Catholic princess Henrietta Maria was also unpopular.

Charles I and Parliament quarrelled over money, religion and Britain's relations with foreign countries. His friendship with the Duke of Buckingham also caused problems. This was because Buckingham involved Britain in unnecessary and expensive wars against Spain and France. To fight the wars, Charles needed money from Parliament which was raised by taxes. This gave Parliament the chance to bargain with the king. Parliament set out a list of their complaints against the king. This was known as the **Petition of Right**. In order to get money from taxes, Charles was forced to agree to the terms of the Petition. However, following the assassination (murder) of the Duke of Buckingham in 1629, relations between Charles and Parliament became worse. Charles dismissed Parliament and did not call it to meet again for eleven years.

The Personal Rule of Charles I 1629–40

Between 1629 and 1640 Charles I ruled the country without calling Parliament. After the years of war, peace was made with France and Spain. This saved money. Also, more money came from the growth of trade between Britain and foreign countries. Thus, Charles and his ministers did not need to ask Parliament for money. During these years, which became known as the **Eleven Years Tyranny**, the king continued to collect taxes which Parliament had agreed to earlier. However, many people were against some of these taxes, and the harsh way in which they were collected. **Ship Money**, for example, which was a tax to support the navy, was very unpopular. To make sure that people obeyed him, Charles used his own special Crown court called the Star Chamber (page 5). Some people were also against Charles for granting **monopoly** rights (for example on the mining of salt) to his favourites at the royal court.

At this time Sir Thomas Wentworth (Earl of Strafford) and William Laud (Archbishop of Canterbury) were the chief advisers to the king. During the 1630s Ireland was controlled by Wentworth and for a time that country seemed both settled and prosperous. However, when Wentworth returned to England, there was a very serious rebellion in Ireland (page 56).

Source C An engraving of Charles I and his son

Gaze on (Fond World) nor wide enough to be
Sway'd by so greate and pure a Maiestee
(Whose Crowne all blisse incircles) that can bring
Health to a Land or Glory to a King.

Investigations

6 In Source **B**, which extract sets out the rights of Parliament? Which extract sets out the power of the monarch? How might the different views cause arguments between the monarch and Parliament?

7 Compare the Royal Arms of the Stuart kings (Source **C**) with the Royal Arms of the Tudors (Source **B**, page 11). What differences can you see ? Which parts of the Arms of the Stuarts show that Charles I was King of England, Scotland and Ireland?

8 In what ways did Charles I want himself and his son to be shown alike? What does this say about Charles I's belief in the hereditary succession of the crown?

9 Why and how did Charles I rule without Parliament for eleven years?

Key words

Subjects People living under the rule of a monarch.
Petition of Right A statement by Parliament of the rights of the people granted by Charles I in 1628.
Eleven Years Tyranny The period, 1629–40, when Charles I ruled without calling Parliament.
Ship Money Money raised through taxes to provide ships for the navy.
Monopoly To have sole control of the making or trade of certain goods.

The Long Parliament

Did Charles rule over a United Kingdom?

Charles I was King of England, Wales, Scotland and Ireland. However, he did not rule over a united kingdom. Not everyone agreed with, or followed, the same religion. Archbishop Laud wanted everyone to follow the ways of the Church of England. This made Laud, and the king, unpopular, especially with the Puritans and the Presbyterians. In 1637 Laud tried to force the Presbyterians in Scotland to use the new version of the English Book of Common Prayer in their churches. This greatly angered the Scots who rose up in revolt.

The Short Parliament

In 1639 the Scots invaded England. Charles I needed money to get an army together to fight them. In 1640 he called Parliament to meet in order to be able to raise money through taxes. However, Parliament said that taxes could not be raised until the king had considered their **grievances**. Charles dismissed Parliament, known as the Short Parliament, after only three weeks.

The Long Parliament

With the Scots still in the north of England, Charles had to call Parliament to meet again. Many members of Parliament were against the king. They would not allow him to raise money through taxes unless he agreed to have less power. There were rumours that Parliament would again be dismissed by the king. Between 1640–1 Parliament introduced important changes to reduce the power of the king. The king's minister, the Earl of Strafford, was **impeached** and beheaded. Archbishop Laud was impeached and imprisoned in the Tower of London. The Court of the Star Chamber was abolished. Some members felt that Parliament had gone far enough. Others wanted to reduce the power of the king even more. When some members

Source B Scottish rioting against the English Prayer Book

> At the outgoing of the church about 30 or 40 of our honestest women, in one voice, before the Bishop and Magistrates, did fall in ... cursing, scolding ... on (the clergyman using the new prayer book) ... (later) ... some hundreds of enraged women ... with fists, and staves, and peats ... beat him sore.

spoke out against the Church of England, Parliament became even more divided in its opinions. The Irish also rose in rebellion in 1641 and thousands of Protestants in Ireland were killed by the Catholic peasantry.

A number of members of Parliament were strongly opposed to the power of Charles I. One of the most important of the king's opponents in the House of Commons was John Pym (1584–1643). Parliament gave Charles I a list of things which they said he had done wrong and which they wanted changed. This list, known as **The Grand Remonstrance**, made the king angry. He took armed men to arrest five of the leading members of the House of Commons, including John Pym, but they all escaped. The king then left London to get an army together so that he could dismiss Parliament. The king raised his standard (flag) at Nottingham. The Civil War was about to begin.

Source C Woodcut showing John Pym

Source D Charles I tries to arrest five members of the House of Commons

Source E The King and the Speaker of the House of Commons – 4 January 1642

Source F
Charles I's Standard

The King: By your leave, Mr Speaker, I must borrow your chair a little. Since I see all the birds are flown, I do expect from you that you shall send them unto me as soon as they return …

The Speaker: May it please your Majesty, I have neither eyes to see nor tongue to speak in this place, but as the House is pleased to direct me.

Investigations

1 Look at Source **A**. The Churchman shown in the pulpit is named in the cartoon. Who is he? What is he trying to read to the people in Church?

2 What might the Churchman in the pulpit (marked 1) write in his report to Archbishop Laud? What might the woman (marked 2) say to her friends about why and how they rioted?

3 Use the information in the text to explain why the riot happened. Why was the use of the new English book of Common Prayer unpopular in Scotland?

4 What was the accusation against John Pym and other members of Parliament?

5 What events led to Charles I entering the House of Commons? Why did the king bring armed men to Parliament with him? Was he successful in his aims?

6 In Source **D** can you see the clerk keeping a record of events (A)? Use the following letter key and the phrases in Source **E** to show what might have been written down in the clerk's book. • The mace holder (B) • the king (C) • the Speaker (D) • the Speaker's Chair (E) • members of the House (F) • the armed men with the King (G).

7 How do the words of the Speaker show that he obeyed the House of Commons rather than the King?

8 Source **F** shows the Standard (flag) of Charles I. Using the information in the source and the text, answer the following questions:
   a) Whose portrait is shown on the Standard?
   b) How does the Standard show that the king ruled England, Scotland and Ireland?
   c) What followed the event shown in Source **F**?

Key words

Grievances Causes or reasons for complaint.
Impeached Accused of a crime, especially treason against the monarch or the country.
The Grand Remonstrance A great protest.

The Civil Wars 1642–9

Who fought in the Civil War?

A Civil War is one in which people living in the same country go to war against each other. From 1642–9 a Civil War took place in England between the supporters of the king and those who supported Parliament. Those on the side of the king were called **Royalists**. They were given the nickname Cavaliers. Those against the king were called **Parliamentarians**. Their nickname was Roundheads. The differences in their appearance and in the clothes they wore, helped to give each side their nicknames.

Who won the Civil War?

The first important battle of the Civil War took place at Edgehill in 1642. Both sides claimed victory. In 1643 Parliament made a treaty with the Scots who sent 20,000 men to fight on the side of the Parliamentarians. In 1644 the Parliamentarians won the important battle of Marston Moor. Shortly afterwards, they captured the city of York, and the Royalists lost much of northern England. The Parliamentarians had formed a **New Model Army** and in 1645 they won another important battle at Naseby. In 1646 Charles I surrendered to the Scots. He was handed over to Parliament and became their prisoner. During the war a Puritan landowner named Oliver Cromwell became an important **general** on the side of the Parliamentarians. Cromwell played an important part in the Parliamentary victories of Marston Moor and Naseby and in forming the New Model Army.

Source A The two sides in the Civil War: a cartoon in 1642

Source B Map showing civil war battles and dates

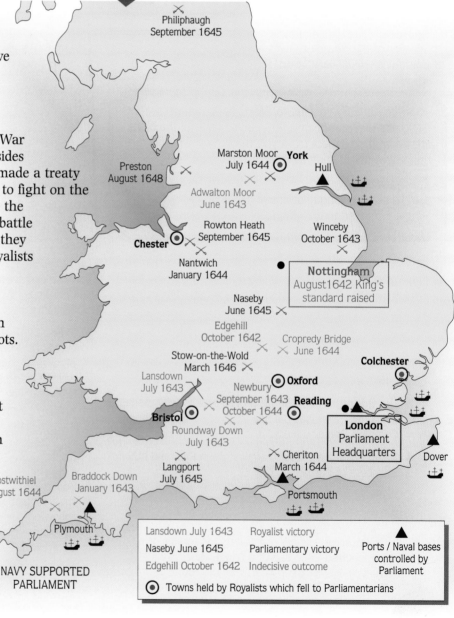

Source C The battle of Marston Moor in 1644

Source D Plan of the battle of Naseby in 1645

Investigations

1 The cartoon (Source **A**) shows two groups on opposite sides in the Civil War. By what nicknames are they known? Describe the clothing, hairstyle and appearance of each group. Can you suggest how each group got its nickname?

2 By what other names were the two groups known? Which group was on the side of the King in the Civil War? Which group was on the side of Parliament?

3 How has the artist made each dog look like its master? How is each side encouraging their dog to behave?

4 Would you say the cartoon was biased (one-sided) or balanced (not supporting either side)? Give reasons for your answer.

5 The map (Source **B**) shows the main battles of the Civil War. The colour code shows which battles were the successes, and which were the defeats of each side. Draw a chart like the one on the right. Then, using the map, record when and where the main battles took place, and for which side it was a victory.

6 Where and when was the first important battle of the Civil War fought?

7 **a)** What battles of the Civil War are shown in Sources **C** and **D**?
b) What were those two battles, and in which years were they fought?
c) Which source do you think is most useful in helping you to understand the battle?

8 What was the name of the Parliamentary general who played an important part in these battles and in the forming of the New Model Army which helped defeat the Royalists?

Date	Royalist victory	Parliamentary victory
1642 ↓		

Depth Study:
The trial and execution of Charles I

In 1647 the king was held in Carisbrooke Castle on the Isle of Wight. While there he made an agreement with the Scots that they would return him to the throne. When the Scots invaded England they were defeated at Preston by an army led by Oliver Cromwell. Parliament had tried to get an agreement with the king about how the country should be governed. However, Cromwell said the king could no longer be trusted. Many Parliamentarians wanted the king to be tried and executed. Cromwell stopped those members who wanted to make peace with the king from entering Parliament. Those members of Parliament who were left were called the **Rump**. They set up a court to try the king. The king said the court did not have the right to try him. Some judges agreed with him. The country was divided between those who wanted Charles back on the throne, and those who did not. The trial of the king lasted four days. He was found guilty of high treason and sentenced to death. On 30 January 1649 Charles I was executed.

Source A Charles I in captivity at Carisbrooke Castle on the Isle of Wight

Source B Charles I as a captive accused of crimes

Rump The group of members of Parliament left after the Long Parliament had been reduced in numbers.

Key words

Source C The trial of Charles I

Investigations

1 Which king is shown in Sources **A** and **B**? Which cartoon favours the king? Which one is against the king? Give reasons for your answer.

2 For what reasons had many of the king's subjects lost their lives during the Civil War? Who is being blamed for this in Source **B**?

3 In Source **B**, the object numbered (1) is a winding (death) sheet or shroud, in which there is a body (2). Whose body is in the winding sheet?

4 Identify the main features of the trial in Westminster Hall (Source **C**) by linking the letter and numbers in the picture with the correct descriptions in the chart below. The letter and first number are done for you.

Feature	Number/letter
Charles Stuart, King of England	A
Chief judge (Lord President)	1
Commissioners who act as judges	
Coat of arms of Parliament (England and Ireland)	
Two Clerks at their table	
The Mace and Sword of State on the table	
The written charge or accusations against the king	
Spectators in galleries	
Soldiers keeping order	
The prosecutor and his two assistants	
The box for the defence counsel (except in treason cases)	

5 The trial scene shows the arms of Parliament (St George of England and the harp of Ireland). Can you suggest why the Royal Arms were not shown in the court?

6 Why is the box marked (10) in the picture empty?

7 Was the court set up because the people of England wanted it or because the army wanted it? Why did Charles I refuse to answer in the court set up to try him?

Source D The charge against Charles Stuart, King of England

T he Charge of the Commons of England against Charles Stuart, King of England, of High Treason and other high crimes ... that he ... is the occasioner ... of the ... cruel, and bloody wars , and ... guilty of all the treasons, murders ... burnings ... damage ... to this nation ...

Source F The Death Warrant of Charles I

Source E King Charles I refuses to accept the authority of the court

I would know by what power I am called hither ... and when I know what lawful authority, I shall answer ... In the meantime ... I have a trust committed to me by God ... I will not betray it to answer to a new unlawful authority.

Source G
The Execution of Charles I

Investigations

8 Identify the main features in Source **G** by linking the numbers in the picture with the correct descriptions in the chart on the right. The first one is done for you.

9 Only one monarch has ever been publicly tried and executed in the country's history. Why did those who executed Charles I want it to take place in public?

10 Why might some people disagree with the execution even though they were against the king?

Feature	Number
The king's chaplain and attendant	
A soldier on the platform supervising the execution	
The king on the execution block	1
The executioner with his axe	
The king's head shown to the crowd	
A portrait of the dead king	
Some of the crowd watching from the roof	
Someone in the crowd who has fainted	
Portraits of Cromwell and one of his generals, Fairfax	

6 The Interregnum

Cromwell and the Commonwealth

After King Charles I was executed in 1649 the country became a **Commonwealth**. This meant that it was a republic, that is a country ruled without a monarch. Nobody had experience of how to govern the country as a **republic**. A number of different ways of governing without a monarch were tried. However, none of them was successful.

The power of the army

The army, under its commander-in-chief Oliver Cromwell, was very powerful at this time. Cromwell was a country gentleman and a Puritan in religion. He had become powerful through his skills as a general in the army. He had been on the side of the Parliamentarians who had defeated the king in the Civil War. For ten years, until his death in 1658, it was Oliver Cromwell, backed by the army, who had the real power in the country.

The numbers of members of Parliament had been reduced (page 52). This smaller Parliament was known as the Rump. When the Rump met after the execution of Charles I it abolished the monarchy and the House of Lords. A **Council of State** was set up to govern the country. This was made up of members of the Rump. The Council depended upon the support of Oliver Cromwell and the army. The new Commonwealth faced a number of dangers and threats.

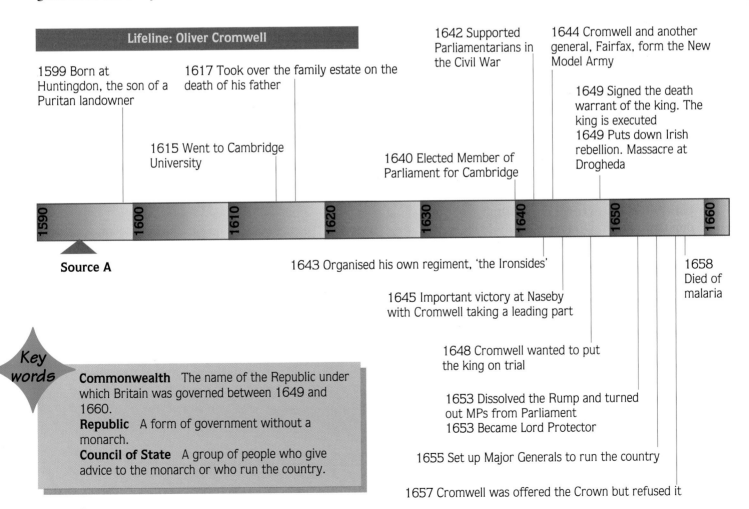

Lifeline: Oliver Cromwell

1599 Born at Huntingdon, the son of a Puritan landowner

1615 Went to Cambridge University

1617 Took over the family estate on the death of his father

1640 Elected Member of Parliament for Cambridge

1642 Supported Parliamentarians in the Civil War

1643 Organised his own regiment, 'the Ironsides'

1644 Cromwell and another general, Fairfax, form the New Model Army

1645 Important victory at Naseby with Cromwell taking a leading part

1648 Cromwell wanted to put the king on trial

1649 Signed the death warrant of the king. The king is executed
1649 Puts down Irish rebellion. Massacre at Drogheda

1653 Dissolved the Rump and turned out MPs from Parliament
1653 Became Lord Protector

1655 Set up Major Generals to run the country

1657 Cromwell was offered the Crown but refused it

1658 Died of malaria

Source A

Key words

Commonwealth The name of the Republic under which Britain was governed between 1649 and 1660.
Republic A form of government without a monarch.
Council of State A group of people who give advice to the monarch or who run the country.

The threat from Ireland

Many Protestants had been killed in Ireland during the 1640s. Many pictures had been published at the time, which had encouraged the English to believe that the Catholics had carried out a wholesale massacre of Protestants. In 1649 there was a Catholic uprising in Ireland. This was a serious threat to the Commonwealth. The Irish said that Charles Stuart, the son of the executed Charles I, was the lawful king. They said he had the right to rule.

Cromwell decided that he would have to put down the Catholic rebellion once and for all. He did so harshly, believing he was doing what God wanted him to do. He showed no mercy. For example, large numbers of people at Drogheda and Wexford in Ireland were massacred by Cromwell's army. Catholic priests were caught and put to death. As a result of Cromwell's **campaign of terror** a large number of the population of Ireland died. Many Irish Catholics were forced off their land, and English Protestants gained more than half the land in Ireland. Cromwell had crushed the Irish uprising but he was hated by the remaining Catholic population. He was known as 'the curse of Ireland'.

Source B The attack on Drogheda

Source C Cromwell's report on the events at Drogheda in a letter to the Speaker of the House of Commons

Dublin, 17 September 1649
Sir,

The army came to the town of Drogheda upon 3 September and upon Monday 9th I asked ... the governor, to surrender the town.

I received no satisfactory answer, and so the guns were used to open ... gaps in the east and south wall.
Upon Tuesday 10th, about five o'clock in the evening, we began the attack and after some hard fighting we entered. The enemy, about seven or eight hundred men, resisted strongly.

Several of the enemy retreated into the Mill Mount, which was very strong and difficult to attack. When our men got to them, they were ordered by me to put all to the sword. In the heat of action, I forbade them (my soldiers) to spare any people who carried weapons in the town.

In the great church called St Peter's near 1000 of them were put to the sword, fleeing there for safety. I think that night they put to the sword in all about 2000 men ... this is the righteous judgement of God upon those barbarous wretches who have dipped their hands in so much innocent blood. This will tend to prevent bloodshed for the future, which is a good enough reason for such action ...

I do not think we lost 100 men, though many be wounded.

Your most obedient servant,
Oliver Cromwell

Source D A Royalist historian (Edward Hyde writing in 1668) describes Drogheda

> The Governor retired into a fort to make conditions to surrender. However, the soldiers were afraid and panicked so that they threw down their weapons when they were offered quarter.
>
> So the enemy entered without resistance and put every man to the sword. They were very cruel and put every soldier to the sword and all the citizens who were Irish, man, woman and child.

The threat from Scotland

Many Scots also believed that Charles Stuart, the son of the executed Charles I, had the right to rule. In 1650 Cromwell's army defeated the Scots at the battle of Dunbar. In 1651, Charles Stuart, his Royalist army, and the Scots were defeated by Cromwell at the battle of Worcester. Charles Stuart escaped. Soon after this Scotland was united to England and Wales. Oliver Cromwell had succeeded in uniting Britain by armed force. The Commonwealth was safe and, for the first time, England, Wales, Ireland and Scotland were joined in a **constitutional** union.

The Anglo–Dutch War

During the 1650s England became a strong **military**, **naval** and trading country. Between 1652 and 1654 England was at war with Holland, over trade. The English navy, commanded by admiral Robert Blake, defeated the Dutch. Both England and Holland were Protestant republics and the two countries soon made peace. (Two other Anglo–Dutch wars occurred in 1665–7 and 1672–4. These were mainly concerned with trade and naval rivalry between England and Holland.)

Rules of siege warfare

- the army leader attacking a town would order the town to surrender

- if the town surrendered before the walls were broken through with cannon fire, the defenders would be given 'quarter' – that is they were not killed or 'put to the sword'

- if the town refused to surrender and was then captured by breaking down the walls with cannon fire and storming in, the defenders could be killed

- in a siege, the defenders could be given 'quarter'. This meant that if they surrendered and gave up their weapons, it was against the rules of war to kill them.

Investigations

1 Why was Ireland seen as a threat to the Commonwealth?

2 What event is shown in Source **B**?

3 What is Source **C** and to whom was it written?

4 Using Sources **B** and **C** can you say which day or days of the siege the artist has shown? How do you know? In Source **C**, how does Cromwell justify putting the inhabitants of Drogheda 'to the sword'?

5 Look at the note on the Rules of Siege Warfare.
   a) Did Cromwell obey the rules? Explain your answer.
   b) As a general, was Cromwell likely to know what might happen if he ordered 'no quarter' for the men in Drogheda?

6 In what ways do Sources **C** and **D** give different accounts of what happened at Drogheda? Can you suggest reasons to explain the differences?

7 **a)** What were Cromwell's views of the Irish people?
   b) How might such views lead to the killing of women and children as well as soldiers?
   c) Why do you think Cromwell became known as 'the curse of Ireland'?

8 Which sources would historians use if they wanted to show Cromwell as a cruel man? Which would they choose if they wanted to show Cromwell as a practical soldier?

Key words

Campaign of terror The harsh use of force which caused great fear among the people affected.
Constitutional To do with the rules by which a country is governed.
Military To do with soldiers or the army.
Naval To do with the navy or ships.

Dangers from religious groups

A number of religious groups, at this time, had new ideas about what society should be like. These included the extreme Puritans who wanted a Puritan republic to run the country, and other groups such as the Levellers, the Fifth Monarchy Men, the Quakers, the Muggletonians and the Ranters. Some groups began to print and circulate pamphlets about their ideas. Although these ideas were only supported by a few people, many other people felt that they were a threat to the government. The Levellers, for example, wanted all adult males to have the vote. They also wanted social reform to help the poor. The Levellers had some support in London and also within the army. When they began to cause trouble in the army, Cromwell **suppressed** them. A number of army Levellers, who were leading a mutiny, were shot.

Source E   A few of the religious groups of the 1640s and 1650s

5 List the different religious groups shown in Source **E**.
  a) How does the print show that people held different kinds of religious beliefs?
  b) Choose three of the groups and write one sentence about each.

6 What other religious groups were active in the seventeenth century?

7 Why were the religious groups a threat to the government?

8 How did Cromwell deal with the threat from the Levellers?

Investigations

Key words   **Suppressed** Put down or held down.

The Protectorate

Why was the Rump dismissed by Cromwell?

Source A Great Seal of England in 1651. The front of the seal is at the top, the back below.

Between 1649 and 1653 the country was governed by the Rump. Cromwell wanted the Rump to pass laws that would give some religious groups the freedom to worship as they wished. He also wanted them to set up elections so that voters could choose who they wanted in a new Parliament. However, the Rump did not do as Cromwell wanted and he dismissed it in 1653. By that time it had become unpopular. The members of the Rump were corrupt and they had failed to lower taxes.

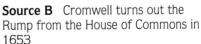

Source B Cromwell turns out the Rump from the House of Commons in 1653

estigations

1 Look at the Great Seal of England (Source **A**).
   a) Which three of the four nations of the British Isles are shown on the front?
   b) Which nation is not shown? Can you explain why?
   c) What scene is shown on the back of the Great Seal?

2 In Source **B**, who is shown as being the most powerful: the Speaker and the members of Parliament or Oliver Cromwell and the army? What does this tell you about who really ruled the country after 1649?

3 Cromwell is shown saying 'Be gone you rogues. You have sat long enough'. To whom is he speaking? When did the Long Parliament first meet (page 48)? When and how did it become the Rump (page 52)?

4 When, and why, was the Rump dismissed by Cromwell? What form of government was set up by Cromwell after the dismissal of the Rump in 1653?

The Lord Protector

Following the dismissal of the Rump in 1653, a new **constitution** (form of government) was drawn up. This made Cromwell the Lord Protector of the country and Commander-in-Chief of the army. He was to govern the country with a council and a Parliament. Only landowners who were not Royalists, Catholics or **Anglicans** were allowed to vote for members of the Parliament.

Religion and social life

Cromwell, as Lord Protector, wanted greater **religious toleration** in the country. For example, for the first time since 1290, Jews were allowed to live in England. Some other groups, for example the Quakers, could hold their own religious services. However, Catholic services were still banned. Protestants could have their own services but they were not allowed to use the Anglican Prayer Book.

The extreme Puritans, who were very powerful at this time, were less tolerant of other religions. They were very strict and liked simple religious services. They had statues and pictures removed from many Anglican churches. They believed that Sunday was a day of rest. People were not allowed to work on that day. They could walk to and from church, but if found on the road for any other reason they could be fined. Theatres were closed down because the Puritans believed that acting and plays were the Devil's work. Other entertainments, such as cock-fighting, bear-baiting, and Maypole dancing were also banned. Holy days, including Christmas Day, were no longer celebrated as religious festivals.

Source C A Puritan pamphlet called *The Lord's Day*, first published in 1639

Source D From a pamphlet in support of Christmas published in 1653

Key words

Constitution The rules by which a monarch or a government run the country.

Anglicans Members of the Church of England.

Religious toleration Allowing people to worship freely.

Major-generals High ranking officers in the army.

Regiment A permanent large group or unit of soldiers.

The rule of the major-generals

Between 1653 and 1658 Oliver Cromwell tried many different ways of governing the country. In 1655 Parliament wanted to increase its own power and tried to reduce the size of the army. Cromwell was against this and decided to try yet another way of running the country. Under this new way, the country was to be ruled by the **major-generals** in the army. The country was divided into 11 districts. Each district was governed by a major-general with the help of a **regiment** of soldiers. In effect, this meant that the country was ruled by Oliver Cromwell and the army. However, the major-generals soon became unpopular. Many landowners and members of Parliament were tired of the harsh rule of the army. In 1657 Parliament presented Cromwell with the Humble Petition and Advice. This suggested that Cromwell should become king and that the House of Lords should be restored. Cromwell knew that the army would not agree to him becoming king, and he refused the Crown.

Source E Oliver Cromwell's Cabinet Councell Discovered (1649)

Investigations

1 The pamphlet (Source **C**) shows ten activities that might be seen on a Sunday: • farming the land • giving bread to the poor • reading the Bible • going to church • dancing • playing cards and games with gambling • drinking and over-eating • visiting the sick • idleness and going to bed too late • getting up early to pray. In two columns, list what Puritans should or should not do on Sunday. The first ones are done for you.

The Puritan Sunday	
Works of light: Puritans should	**Works of darkness: Puritans should not**
• Get up early and pray	• Be idle and go to bed too late
To be completed	

Use the information to complete a chart like the one below. Write out a Sunday timetable in the life of a Puritan. Then write out the details of a modern Sunday.

Example	**A Puritan Sunday in the seventeenth century**	**My Sunday today 199–**
Time	Sunrise	
Activity	Get up and say prayers	
Time		
Activity		
To be completed		

2 How do you explain the differences between a Puritan Sunday and your Sunday? Are there any similarities?

3 The Puritans banned the celebration of Christmas. Why did the ban prove very unpopular? How does the drawing show that country people were more likely than town people to want to keep the old ways?

4 Between 1649 and 1653 the country was governed by the Council of State. Can you find the following in Source **E**:
a) two small devil-like figures on either side of the Arms of England and Ireland?
b) the curtains being opened to reveal (discover) 'Oliver Cromwell's Cabinet Council'?
c) the devil (A) in the chair?
d) members of the council co-operating with the devil, including Cromwell (B) and John Bradshaw (C) the chief judge at Charles I's trial?

5 What do you think the cartoon is trying to say? Do you think it was produced by the Royalists or the Parliamentarians? Explain your answer.

Source G   Historian's interpretation of Cromwell by S. R. Gardiner

> The National hero ... the greatest because the most typical Englishman of all time.

Source H   Historian's interpretation of Cromwell by C. V. Wedgwood

> His cruelty and ruthlessness have left a mark and a memory that the last three hundred years have not been able to wipe out ...

Why was the monarchy restored?

When Oliver Cromwell died in 1658, his son Richard took his place. However, Richard Cromwell was neither a soldier nor a **statesman**. There were arguments between Parliament and the army and Richard Cromwell could not control them. The Rump Parliament met and forced him to give up power.

People had had enough of the republic and wanted the return of the monarchy. An army general called George Monck said the army should obey Parliament. Monck marched on London to prepare the way for the return of the monarchy. Parliament asked Charles Stuart to return as king. Charles made an agreement called the Declaration of Breda. This promised that the balance of power between Parliament and the Crown would be sorted out. In 1660 Charles II became king. The monarchy had been restored.

Key words

Statesman   A person who is skilled in politics or in the affairs of running the country.

Investigations

3 Using the text and Cromwell's lifeline explain Source **F** by answering the following questions:
   a) Why is Cromwell shown in armour and carrying a sword?
   b) How had Cromwell become powerful?
   c) How did he keep his power?

4 a) In what ways does the picture show that Cromwell believed he had God's support?
   b) In the right hand pillar England, Scotland and Ireland can be seen holding out victory wreaths. To whom are they offering them, and why?
   c) Cromwell holds three crowns on his sword. Which nations do they represent? How had he brought the three nations together?

5 Cromwell believed he had brought peace and happiness to the country. Which occupations can be seen enjoying this?
   a) The picture shows Cromwell bringing peace through the use of force. What are the symbols of peace and the symbols of force?

6 How is Cromwell shown trampling on Roman Catholicism?

7 Is Cromwell shown as a powerful or weak person? Support your answer with information from the picture.

8 Explain how the writers of Sources **G** and **H** could hold such different views about Cromwell? Explain how it might be possible for both views to be correct.

9 Cromwell's statue stands guard outside Parliament today. From all you have learned about Cromwell, say whether or not you think he deserves this position, and why?

7 The Restoration Age

The return to monarchy

What was restored with the return of the monarchy?

On 29 May 1660, Charles II returned to London. Large crowds turned out to welcome him, and church bells were rung throughout the country. Charles II was an intelligent man. He was easy to get on with. During his time in exile he had learned how to survive. He was determined never to be exiled from his country again. Most people were glad that the harsh rule of Cromwell and the army was over. They were pleased that they would, once again, be able to enjoy the kinds of entertainment that had been banned during the **Interregnum**.

Source A News of the Restoration from Pepys' diary

2 May 1660:
Welcome news of the Parliament's votes yesterday, which will be remembered for the happiest Mayday that hath been ... Great joy all yesterday at London, and at night more bonfires than ever, and ringing of bells, and drinking of the king's health upon their knees in the streets ...

13 May 1660:
The tailors and painters were at work, cutting out some pieces of yellow cloth in the fashion of a crown and C. R., and put it ... into the flag instead of the state's arms ... the Harp must be taken out of all their flags, it being very offensive to the King.

Source B The coronation procession of Charles II in 1661

Source C Pepys describes the arrival of Charles II at Dover on the king's return to England

25 May:
The King ... was received by General Monk [Monck] with ... love and respect at ... Dover. Infinite the crowd of people and ... the horsemen, citizens and noblement ... and so into a stately coach and away towards Canterbury ... The shouting and joy expressed by all is past imagination.

Investigations

1 a) What had to take place in Parliament before the monarchy could be restored?
b) Why were many people glad to see the Restoration of the monarchy?
c) How might the Restoration affect the everyday lives of ordinary people?

2 Explain why the design of flags and coats of arms had to be changed at this time? Which country had the symbol of the Harp? Why was it removed from the flags?

Key words

Interregnum An interval or period between reigns. When normal government is suspended usually between reigns.

> *29 May*:
>
> **A** bonfire for joy of the day, it being the King's birthday ... This day it is thought the King do enter the city of London.

Source E Oliver Cromwell's head

The restored monarchy was not as powerful as it had been in Tudor times (page 9). Charles II did not want to fall out with Parliament or the Church. Neither did he want revenge for what had happened to his father. Thus only 50 Parliamentary leaders were punished for taking part in the Civil War and in the trial and execution of Charles I. Only 11 of these were executed. However, Oliver Cromwell's body was dug up and hanged before a large crowd. His head was put on a pole and shown in public. The Royalists who had had their lands and property taken from them, wanted it back when they returned from exile. However, if the Royalists had sold their property, they did not get it back.

How did Charles II work with Parliament?

In 1660 the House of Lords was restored (brought back). Its members were Royalist nobles, and bishops of the Church of England. Charles could choose his own ministers and advisers. He could also decide when to call Parliament to meet. However, Parliament could talk about how the money they granted the king was spent. This gave Parliament some control over the government. When Parliament refused to give the king enough money to run the government and the royal household, Charles reached an agreement with them. Charles was also helped by the fact that many people feared that the country might become a republic again. However, the king's power was limited by Parliament in other ways. They also opposed his efforts to bring about religious toleration in the country.

When Charles II was restored to the throne, the Church of England once again became the established Church. The Church disliked the Puritans but could not get rid of them. Acts were passed by Parliament against **non-conformists**, that is those who did not **conform** to, or follow the rules of, the Church of England. As a result of the Test Act of 1673, members of the Church of England had to show that they supported the beliefs of the Church. For example, school teachers had to prove that they received the **sacraments**. The clergy also had to promise that they would follow Church of England services. Catholics and non-conformists were excluded from public office.

Investigations

4 Which of the following reasons do you think explains why Oliver Cromwell's head was put on a pole and shown in public:
- for revenge,
- as an example, to show what might happen to those who opposed the monarch, or
- to remind people that Cromwell was dead?

5 What other actions were taken against those blamed for the trial and execution of Charles I?

6 Write three sentences describing Charles II as he is shown in his portrait (Source **F**). Charles II was interested in ships and navigation. How is this shown in the portrait?

7 What is the link between this portrait (Source **F**) and the portrait (Source **C**, page 47)? What is the family relationship between the people shown?

8 Why was the power of the restored monarchy not as great as it had been in Tudor times?

9 In Source **G** the king can be seen touching some of his subjects who were ill with a disease called scrofula which caused dangerous swellings of the glands. Was this:
- to bless them before they died
- to try to cure them by his touch
- to protect himself against the disease?

Key words

Non-conformists Those who did not belong (or conform to) the Church of England.
Conform To follow or obey the rules.
Sacrament An act or ceremony of the Christian churches which is an outward or visible sign of inward grace.

The Great Plague of 1665

- ● **What is bubonic plague?**
- ● **What are the symptoms of bubonic plague?**

Bubonic plague is a disease. It is caused by **bacteria** (germs). The bacteria are carried by fleas which live in the fur of black rats. Plague is spread to humans when they are bitten by the fleas. However, it was not until 1894 that scientists discovered that this was the real cause of the disease.

People with bubonic plague become ill with a fever and a very high temperature. Symptoms of the disease include sneezing, a pink rash and painful swellings on the body which turn black.

What was the Great Plague?

In 1665 there was an outbreak of plague in London. Plague was not a new disease. There had been outbreaks in England and Europe many times before, and many people had died. The crowded and unhealthy conditions in which some people lived meant that the plague of 1665 spread quickly. The cases of plague, and the number of deaths, increased during the hot summer months.

30 April: Great fear of the sickness ... two or three houses are already shut up...

7 June: The hottest day that ever I felt in my life ... I did ... see two or three houses marked with a red cross upon the doors.

15 June: The town grows very sickly, and people to be afraid of it; there dying this last week of the plague 112 ...

29 June: Waggons and people ready to go out of town ... The Mortality Bill is come to 267.

13 July: Above 700 died of the plague this week.

20 July: Dying 1089 ... this week ... Lord! to see how the plague spreads!

3 August: The plague is ... this week ... 2020.

10 August: This week rise so high, to ... above 3000 of the plague.

31 August: In the city died this week ... 6102 of the plague.

7 September: Dead ... 6978 of the plague.

31 October: Number of deaths ... of the plague 1031.

22 November: The plague is ... 600 ...

30 November: Great joy we have ... but 333 of the plague ...

31 December: The plague is ... almost to nothing ... the town fills. Shops begin to be open again.

Source B Extract from Bill of Mortality

What did people think caused the plague?

People blamed many different things for causing bubonic plague. Some felt that it was sent by God as a punishment for wrong doing. Many believed it was caused by the bad air and the nasty smells in the dirty London streets. Others said it came from cats and dogs. At this time, the true cause of the plague was not known.

What did people do to protect themselves from plague?

As the plague spread, many people fled from London to live in the countryside. Others carried sweet-smelling flowers and herbs to protect themselves from the bad smells which they thought caused the disease. A red cross was painted on the doors of those houses where there was plague, to warn healthy people to keep away. Sometimes those with plague were taken to a pest or plague house and kept there. Many thousands of people died of plague in 1665. The dead were put on carts and carried away at night. When they were taken to be buried a bell was rung to warn people. Often such large numbers of people died that many bodies had to be buried together in one large grave.

Source C The plague and its consequences

Multituds flying from London by water in boats & barges

Flying by land

Burying the dead with a bell before them.   Searchers.

Carts full of dead to bury.

Investigations

1 **a)** What is the cause of bubonic plague?
   b) How did people think it was caused in the seventeenth century?
   c) How might these differences in knowledge have made it difficult to treat outbreaks of Plague in 1665 and stop it spreading?

2 Use the information in Source **A** to work out:
   • in which season of the year the outbreak began,
   • in which season of the year the plague was worst,
   • in which months most people died of the disease,
   • when the plague began to die down.

3 Source **B** is a Bill of Mortality. Every week a new Bill gave the number of deaths and the causes. How many people were buried in London in the week 15–22 August 1665? Of these how many died of plague. What percentage or proportion of deaths was due to plague?

4 **a)** How many parishes were clear of plague?
   b) How many were affected by the plague?
   c) What percentage of London parishes were affected by plague?
   d) What do the percentages tell you about how serious plague was in August 1665?

5 Source **B** provides official information. Samuel Pepys diary also provides information for the month of August. Compare the two sources. Where might Pepys have got his information from?

6 **a)** In what ways, and why, are people shown leaving London in Source **C**?
   b) How might the movement of people help the plague to spread?
   c) Why might the government (Source **D**) want to stop people from leaving London?

Key words

Bacteria Germs which, when in a person's body, cause illness or disease.

Source D Trying to prevent the spread of the plague

I t was rumoured that an Order of the Government was to ... place turnpikes and barriers on the road to prevent people's travelling and ... people from London to pass, for fear of bringing the infection along with them.

Daniel Defoe, *A Journal of the Plague Year* (1722)

Source E Some problems with burying the dead

T he cart had in it sixteen or seventeen bodies ... to be huddled together into the common grave of mankind ... rich and poor went together. There was no other way of burials ... for coffins were not to be had for the ... numbers that fell in such a calamity as this.

Daniel Defoe, *A Journal of the Plague Year* (1722)

What treatment might be given to people with the plague?

Because the real cause of the plague was not known, the treatments used to try to cure it did not work. Plague doctors wore gloves and beak-shaped masks filled with perfume to protect themselves from infection. They used such things as toads and blood-sucking leeches to treat the disease but without success.

When and why did the plague die down?

As the weather became colder in the winter months, the numbers of cases of plague fell. By the end of 1665 the worst of the disease was over, although there were still a few cases. A number of reasons have been suggested as to why the plague eventually died down. These include the colder weather, and the decline of black rats which were slowly replaced by brown rats which lived in the drains and sewers rather than in houses.

Investigations

7 What problems were there in burying the dead?

8 Using the information in Sources **C** and **E**, explain how these problems were dealt with.

9 Describe the costume of the plague doctor. Why did they dress in this way? In what ways did they think the costume would protect them from the plague?

10 Samuel Pepys wrote his diary (Source **A**) at the time of the Plague. Daniel Defoe wrote his novel *A Journal of the Plague Year* (Sources **D** and **E**) in 1722. Which sources do you think are most reliable, and why?

Source F Costume worn by doctors to protect them from the plague

Depth Study:
The Great Fire of London 1666

What was the Great Fire?

On Sunday, 2 September 1666 a fire began in London. It is said to have started in a baker's shop in Pudding Lane, shortly after midnight. It spread quickly through the streets and buildings of London. It was not until Thursday, 6 September that the fire was finally put out.

Source A London burning by day

Source B Pepys records the Great Fire in his diary

September 2 (1666):

About 3 in the morning ... a great fire ... began ... in the King's baker's house, in Pudding Lane ... the fire rage every way; and nobody ... endeavouring (trying) to quench it, but to remove their goods, and leave all to the fire ... the wind mighty high and driving it into the city; and everything after so long a drought ... combustible.

Investigations

1 Why might the fire shown in Source **A** be described as a 'Great Fire'? Using Sources **A** and **B**, can you:
   - explain in which direction the wind was blowing,
   - say what stopped the fire spreading south,
   - give the name of the river?

2 Using Source **B** explain why the fire became a Great Fire. Include the following in your answer:
   - day and time of the outbreak,
   - people's actions,
   - weather conditions at the time and over the past weeks.

Why and how did it become a 'Great Fire'?

Outbreaks of small fires in towns were common. However, there were a number of reasons why the small fire in the baker's shop became a 'Great Fire'. The summer of 1666 had been hot in London. The wooden buildings were very dry. At the time of the fire, there was a strong wind blowing from the east. The wind fanned the flames which spread across the city in a westerly direction. Sparks from the fire were carried by the wind. These set fire to other buildings. There were also many difficulties in fighting the fire and in trying to put it out.

How did people try to fight the Great Fire?

At the time of the Great Fire, there was no proper fire brigade such as we have today. Water used to put out fires had to be carried in leather buckets. Fire syringes were used to squirt water on to the fire. However, there was a shortage of water in the areas where the fire burned. Large fire-hooks were used to pull down the buildings in the path of the fire. This was meant to stop the fire spreading. However, buildings caught fire faster than people could pull them down. Finally, it was decided to blow up the buildings to make gaps so that the fire could not spread across them easily.

How did people try to save themselves?

When people began to realise how dangerous the fire was, they feared for their lives and property. Some loaded their belongings on to carts and left London. Some people put themselves and their belongings on to boats to cross the river Thames to safety. Others buried their treasure under the ground, hoping it would not be destroyed by the fire.

Source C A fire engine from the time of the Great Fire of London

Source D Pepys advises other ways of stopping the Great Fire

> I did tell the King and the Duke of York ... that unless His Majesty ... command houses to be pulled down nothing could stop the fire

Source E Pepys records in his diary how he tried to save his goods

> Did by moonshine ... carry much of my goods into the garden ... and my money and iron chests into my cellar ... and got my bags of gold ... ready to carry away, and my chief papers of accounts also ...

Did the Great Fire do much damage?

St Paul's Cathedral was destroyed in the Great Fire, together with about 90 other churches. Other important buildings were also burned down. These included the Royal Exchange, the Guildhall, Newgate Gaol and a number of Company Halls. Over 13,000 houses were destroyed and about 100,000 people lost their homes. Although the loss of belongings and property was great, very few people lost their lives in the fire.

The rebuilding of London

After the Great Fire of 1666 much of London was rebuilt in brick or stone. A famous architect, called Sir Christopher Wren (1632–1723) was appointed as Surveyor General. Wren's main job was to see that the churches in London were rebuilt.

The re-building of St. Paul's Cathedral was begun in 1675 and completed in 1710. Fifty other London churches, including St Mary le Bow, were also rebuilt. Wren's buildings stand today as examples of the architectural achievements of the time (page 102).

Source G   St Paul's Cathedral today

Source F   Portrait of Sir Christopher Wren

Investigations

3 Explain how you think the fire engine shown in Source **C** worked. How was the engine moved about? Where was the water kept and how was it used?

4 How useful would the engine be in putting out a fire such as that shown in Source **A**?

5 What way of fighting the fire proved more successful than the use of the fire engine?

6 Why did people try to take their goods out of London? How might the possessions that people tried to save tell you something about them?

7 Which of his possessions did Samuel Pepys try to save, and how? Do you think he would have tried to 'save' his diary? What six possessions would you save in the event of a fire?

8 Why did much of London have to be rebuilt after 1666? Why was stone and brick used for rebuilding rather than wood?

9 Can you explain why Christopher Wren (Source **F**) is shown holding a plan of St Paul's Cathedral? What famous building is shown in the painting and why was Wren proud of it?

10 How do you know from the evidence in the portrait that Wren was an astronomer?

11 Explain why Wren's interest in mathematics and geometry might be useful in his work in rebuilding London.

12 Name and describe the building shown in Source **G**. Look up and use the following words if you wish.

cathedral   dome   columns   pediments
balustrades   classical   towers

13 Where can you visit this building today, and what is its purpose?

71

8 The Revolution of 1688 and its consequences

The reign of James II 1685–8

After the death of Charles II in 1685, his younger brother James II (James VII of Scotland) became king. James was a skilled soldier and sailor. During the reign of his brother he had served his country well. However James II was king for only three years, from 1685–8. After one of the shortest reigns in British history, he was removed from the throne in what became known as the **Glorious Revolution**. This chapter is about the causes and the events which led to the removal of James II from the throne. It is also about his replacement by his daughter Mary and her husband, William of Orange. Finally, it is about the causes and results of the Revolution of 1688 and its effects on the making of the United Kingdom.

Source A Portrait of James Stuart (James II) by Sir Godfrey Kneller

The Monmouth Rebellion

James II was a convert to the Catholic religion and not everyone wanted him to become king. Some years earlier, during the reign of Charles II, some members in Parliament (who became known as **Whigs**) had tried to pass a **Bill** called the Exclusion Bill. The Bill was intended to stop, that is exclude, James from becoming king. However, the Bill was defeated by other Royalists in Parliament (who became known as **Tories**). The illegitimate son of Charles II, who was called the Duke of Monmouth, also wanted to become king. He tried to get people to accept him as the lawful heir of King Charles. This led to him being **banished** from Britain. When James II became king in 1685, Monmouth returned to England to claim the throne. The Monmouth Rebellion had the support of some Protestants but most people supported James II as the lawful king. James's army defeated Monmouth at the battle of Sedgemoor, in Somerset. Monmouth was captured and executed.

How did James lose the support of his people?

When James became king he tried to increase his own power and that of his ministers. This worried Parliament and many of the people in the country. He also lost the support of many of his subjects because of his strong Catholic beliefs. In 1687 James made a **Declaration**. This was known as the Declaration of Indulgence. It abolished the harsh laws which had been passed by Parliament against non-conformists (that is those people who did not support the Church of England). Although the Declaration of Indulgence gave rights to Protestant non-conformists as well as to Catholics, many people were suspicious of James's intentions. They feared that he might want to bring the country back to Roman Catholicism. At the same time the king also gave Catholics important positions in government, the Church and the Universities. Many people were against the Declaration, including seven Church of England bishops who were put on trial but found not guilty. When it became known that King James and his queen, Mary of Modena, were expecting a child, many people became alarmed. They feared that there would be a long line of future Catholic monarchs.

Key words

Glorious Revolution A term used to describe the events that led to the removal of James II from the English throne and his replacement by his daughter Mary and her husband William of Orange.

Whigs A term given to those who opposed James, Duke of York, becoming king, on the ground of his being Roman Catholic. The Whigs were supporters of the 1688 Revolution and believed that power should lie with Parliament.

Bill During its passage through the House of Commons and the House of Lords a proposed law is known as a Bill. If a Bill is approved by Parliament and the monarch it becomes an Act of Parliament.

Tories The group in Parliament who opposed the Whigs. The Tories were strong supporters of the Church of England.

Banished Made to go, or sent to live, in another country.

Declaration A strong statement about something

Investigations

1 How had James served his country before he became king?

2 How does Source **A** show that James wanted to be seen as a successful soldier and sailor?

3 The portrait was originally painted before James became king. The portrait was added to and changed after James became king. What two important additions were made to the picture?

4 The portrait was the work of a famous painter. He was well known for being able to 'show' the personality of those he painted. Write down ONE word which you think best describes the personality of James II. Then compare your word with those of all members of the class. Which words are used most often?

5 In what way might the personality of a king affect the way he ruled the country? How did the personality of James II affect the events which led to his removal from the throne?

The Revolution of 1688

What were the reasons for the revolution of 1688?

There were a number of causes of the revolution of 1688. James II was an unpopular king. Many important men in Parliament and in the Church of England disliked the way he tried to increase his own power. People also feared that the king was trying to bring back Roman Catholicism to the country. These fears were made worse by the fact that Britain's neighbour, France, was a Catholic country. France was ruled by Louis XIV, the most powerful Catholic king in Europe.

Was there an alternative to having James II as king?

William of Orange, a Protestant prince, was the leader of the Dutch people in Holland. The Dutch people, like the English, mainly followed the Protestant religion. William was an enemy of the Catholic king, Louis XIV of France. Both William of Orange and his wife Mary were related to the British monarchy. William was the grandson of Charles I, and Mary was the Protestant daughter of James II and his first wife Anne Hyde. Important Protestant members in the Britsh parliament, who feared and disliked James II, began to think about replacing him as king. They said that William and Mary had a claim to the English throne.

Source A A cartoon of the time showing how the Protestant family of Orange saved England

How did William and Mary become king and queen?

In 1688 the Whig members of Parliament, and some Tories, sent a letter to the Dutch Protestant prince, William of Orange. They asked William to come to England with an army, so that he and his wife Mary could become king and queen in place of James II. William landed in England at Torbay in Devon with a large army. He marched towards London gathering support on the way. James II fled to France.

Source B The landing of William of Orange with a Dutch army in 1688

5 November, 1688:

I went to London and heard the news of the Prince (of Orange) having landed at Torbay. He came with a fleet of near 700 sail, passing through the Channel with so favourable a wind, that our navy could not intercept ... them. This put the King and Court into great consternation ...

18 December, 1688:

I saw the King take barge ... a sad sight! The Prince (of Orange) ... fills Whitehall with Dutch guards.

Source C John Evelyn records the events of 1688 in his diary

Investigations

1 How does the cartoon suggest that the Pope, Louis XIV of France, James II and the English Catholics (numbers 1, 2, 3 and 4) were threats to England. How does it show that the Protestant Church of England (B) had been almost overturned in the reign of James II?

2 The eye of God (A) sees the dangers facing England. A favourable wind (C) blows William of Orange (D) to save England. What is the message in the cartoon?

3 Look back to Source **D** in Chapter 3 (page 37). What similarities can you see between that cartoon and Source **A** on page 74?

4 Can you say:
a) Which country was seen as the main danger to Britain in the late seventeenth century?
b) Which country had been the main danger to Britain in the late sixteenth century?
c) What was the main religion of those two countries (France and Spain)?
d) What was the main religion in Britain?
e) What was the religion of William of Orange?

5 How does the cartoon show the Orange family? Can you suggest why the tree includes a number of coats of arms of the house of Orange?

6 In what way is the cartoon biased (one-sided)?

7 Sources **B** and **C** are about the same event. What is it? How does the picture source provide different kinds of information to the written source?

8 Which of the sources tells you how long it took for the invading army to reach London?

9 How could a wind blowing from the east or north east favour William's invasion fleet sailing from Holland? How could the same wind keep James II's fleet at anchor in the river Thames? Why was this called 'the Protestant wind'?

10 The events of 1688 are called a 'revolution'. Find out the meaning of the word revolution? Is it the right word to use to describe the events of 1688? Explain your answer.

Ireland

How was Ireland brought under Protestant control?

The **deposed** king, James II, tried to get back his throne by using Ireland as a base. When James landed in Ireland he got some support from a Catholic Irish army. A number of towns, including Londonderry, were **besieged** by the Catholic forces. After a **siege** of four months, Londonderry was freed by the English fleet. In 1690, William III and his English army defeated James at the battle of the Boyne. Once more, James was forced to flee to France.

The English victory at the battle of the Boyne meant that Ireland became little more than a British **colony**. Parliament passed a number of Acts against the Catholics in Ireland. Catholics were not allowed to vote in parliamentary elections. They could not have jobs in national or local government. They were also forbidden from wearing swords, the symbol of a gentleman. A Protestant **oligarchy** controlled the Irish Parliament. The Protestants owned most of the land and controlled industry and trade. Ireland was governed from Dublin Castle, helped by an English army. The Catholics had no political power and were largely under the control of the Protestant **minority**.

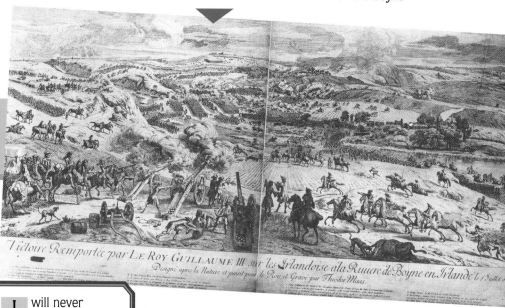

Source A The battlefield of the Boyne

> I will never command an Irish army again! I must shift for myself and so must you.

Source B James Stuart after the defeat at the Boyne

The consequences of the Revolution of 1688

After the 1688 Revolution, William and Mary were crowned as joint monarchs. However, before they were crowned they agreed to Parliament having important rights. This was called the Declaration of Rights. It was passed in Parliament as the Bill of Rights in 1689. The **Bill of Rights** meant that, in future, Parliament would have more power. Everyone, except for Catholics, was given the freedom to worship in the ways of their chosen religion.

The Bill of Rights said that:

- Parliament should meet often.
- Members of Parliament could speak freely on all matters.
- Parliament should control taxes
- Parliament should make laws.

Key words

Deposed Removed from power.
Besieged To lay siege to, for example a town or city.
Siege Surrounding a place with armed forces, for example a town or city, and preventing people or goods from entering or leaving.
Colony Territory or country which is run by the government of another country.
Oligarchy Government or the running of a country by a small group of people.
Minority The smaller part of a group.
Bill of Rights A statement of the rights of a group of people. A law passed by the English Parliament in 1689.

Investigations

1 Where and when did the battle of the Boyne take place?

2 Who led the Irish army? Who led the English army? Which side won the battle?

3 What information does Source **A** provide about the battle of the Boyne?

4 What happened to the Catholics in Ireland following the English victory?

5 Which parts of the United Kingdom still celebrate the battle of the Boyne and why?

Depth Study: Scotland

Who were the Jacobites in Scotland?

In 1603 the Crowns of England and Scotland had been united under the Stuart monarchy (page 25). However, the Scottish people did not share fully in the growing wealth of Britain. There was very little industry in Scotland and the country stayed poor in many ways. The Navigation Acts passed by the English Parliament prevented Scottish traders and shipping from trading with England's growing **empire**. After the Revolution of 1688 a small number of Scots continued to support the deposed king, James II. These supporters were called the **Jacobites**.

The Jacobites, who supported the claims of James II, lived mainly in the Scottish Highlands. In 1689–90, William III defeated the Jacobites in Scotland. The Scottish clans were ordered to take an oath of loyalty to William and Mary. Most did so. However, the Catholic MacDonald clan did not take the oath until five days after the deadline. This provided an excuse for the soldiers of the Campbell clan to punish the MacDonalds. The soldiers, acting on the orders of the government, massacred about forty of the MacDonald clan at Glencoe in 1692.

Source A The Glencoe Massacre as painted in Victorian times

Empire A number of countries (colonies) ruled by one government.
Jacobites Supporters of James II of England (James VII of Scotland) and his Catholic descendants after the Revolution of 1688.

Key words

Who was to be the next monarch after William III?

In 1694, Mary died and William continued to rule the country. In 1701, the Act of Settlement was passed. This said that the Catholic **descendants** of James II could not succeed to the British throne. Instead, the crown would go to Anne, the *Protestant* daughter of James II. As a result of the Act, only Protestants would be able to sit on the throne of Britain in future. Should Anne die childless, the throne would pass to the Protestant princes of Hanover in Germany.

In the same year that the Act of Settlement was passed, 1701, the deposed king, James II died in exile in France. His son, James Edward Stuart (known as the **Old Pretender**), and later his grandson Charles Edward Stuart (known as the **Young Pretender**) continued to claim the British throne. When William III died in 1702, the crown passed to Queen Anne (1702–14).

Source B Family tree: the later Stuarts and Hanoverians

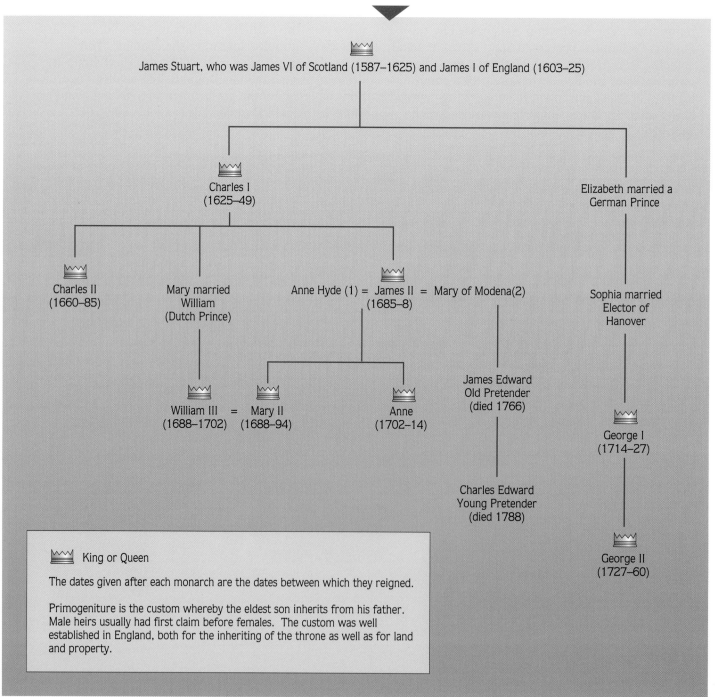

King or Queen

The dates given after each monarch are the dates between which they reigned.

Primogeniture is the custom whereby the eldest son inherits from his father. Male heirs usually had first claim before females. The custom was well established in England, both for the inheriting of the throne as well as for land and property.

Why did the English and Scottish Parliaments unite in 1707?

The long European wars, in which Britain, Holland and their allies fought against France, harmed the trade of Scotland. A growing number of Scots wanted a share in England's trade with her Empire. Also, at this time, the English Parliament was afraid that the Scottish Parliament might not support the English Act of Settlement of 1701 (page 78). Although Queen Anne had many children, they had all died. Scotland and England had been united under the same royal family since 1603. Difficulties might arise if the two countries were ruled by different royal families.

Both the Scottish and the English Parliaments saw that there were benefits if the two Parliaments united. Those in Scotland who were against Union were bribed to support an Act uniting the two Parliaments. The 1707 Act of Union ended the Scottish Parliament in Edinburgh. The Act said that 45 Scots MPs and 16 lords were to represent Scotland in the Parliament at Westminster. Although the English and Scottish Parliaments were united, the Scots kept control over law and education in Scotland. The Scots also kept their own (Presbyterian) Church. Union between the two countries meant that Scotland could trade fully with Britain's empire.

Why were the Jacobites defeated?

At first the 1707 Union provided little benefit for many parts of Scotland. In particular, the Highlands of Scotland stayed poor. The Highlands were the main areas where the Jacobites supported the claims of the Catholic Pretenders (James Edward Stuart and later Charles Edward Stuart) to the throne. There were a number of rebellions in support of the Pretenders. Jacobite rebellions in 1708, 1715 and 1745 were also supported by some Scots who were unhappy about the Union.

In 1715 there was a serious Jacobite uprising in support of James Edward Stuart, the Old Pretender. Although successful at first the rebellion was eventually defeated. In 1745 Charles Edward Stuart, the Young Pretender, led another Jacobite rebellion. However, only a few of the Highland clans supported him. The rebels took Edinburgh and invaded England as far south as Derby. However, the Jacobites then decided to retreat. The Jacobite rebellion was finally defeated at the battle of Culloden in 1746, the last battle to be fought in Britain. Many more Highlanders and their families were later killed by the British army. After several weeks on the run, the Young Pretender escaped to France. The National Anthem first made its appearance at this time, beginning 'God save great George our King'.

Flora Macdonald (1722–90), who helped the Young Pretender to escape by disguising him as her maid, was imprisoned for a short time. She has earned a place in history as a Scottish heroine.

Investigations

1 What events led up to the massacre at Glencoe?

2 Sometimes factual or 'true' history gets mixed up with legends or folk history. Sometimes legends or stories which are retold many times may become exaggerated. After the events at Glencoe there were many stories about the bravery of the Campbell clan and the treachery of those who had carried out the massacre.

3 How and why might an event such as the massacre at Glencoe become part of Scottish folk history?

4 How and why might later paintings of such events provide an image of what happened rather than the reality?

5 Look at the family tree. Choose from the following relationships: sister, brother-in-law, half-brother, father to say what relation Queen Anne was to each of these people: • James II • Mary the wife of William of Orange and queen 1688–94 • William of Orange • James Edward Stuart (the Old Pretender).

6 According to the custom of primogeniture who do you think had the best claim to the throne after the death of William III in 1702: James Edward Stuart, or Anne? Which of the two became monarch?

7 Who had the best claim to the throne in 1714: James Edward Stuart, or George of Hanover? Which of the two became monarch?

8 Who claimed to be the rightful ruler after the death of Queen Anne? Which Act of Parliament meant that he could not inherit the throne?

Key words

Descendants A person or persons descended from an ancestor.

Old Pretender A pretender is a person who claims a throne or title. The Old Pretender was the son of James II and Mary of Modena.

Young Pretender The son of the Old Pretender.

Source C Map of Britain in 1745–6

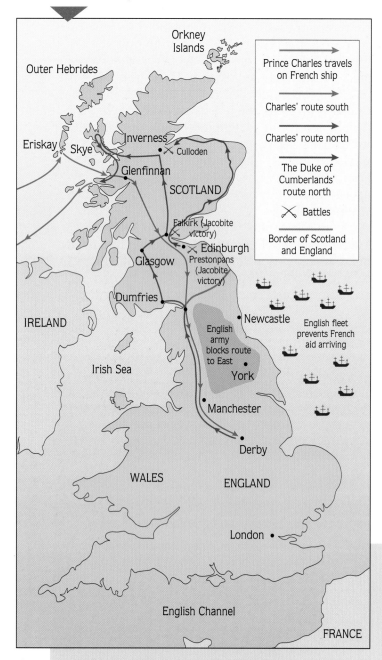

Legend:
- Prince Charles travels on French ship
- Charles' route south
- Charles' route north
- The Duke of Cumberlands' route north
- ✕ Battles
- Border of Scotland and England

Map labels: Orkney Islands, Outer Hebrides, Eriskay, Skye, Inverness, ✕ Culloden, Glenfinnan, SCOTLAND, Falkirk (Jacobite victory), Edinburgh, Glasgow, Prestonpans (Jacobite victory), Dumfries, IRELAND, Irish Sea, Newcastle, English fleet prevents French aid arriving, English army blocks route to East, York, Manchester, Derby, WALES, ENGLAND, London, English Channel, FRANCE

Source D

Causes of the Jacobite rising in 1745

1 Many Scots disliked Act of Union

2 Money was given by a Scottish banker living in France

3 Old Pretender, seen as lawful heir of James II

4 Many Scots disliked paying taxes to government in London

5 Old and New Pretenders were Catholics as were many Scottish Highland clans

6 Many Scots against James II being deposed

7 Belief that George II had no right to be king

8 Belief that France would give some support to Jacobite rebellions

9 After 1707 Act of Union, series of Jacobite plots to put Stuarts back on the throne

10 Act of Union was unpopular. Some people in Scotland wanted a separate Parliament

11 After defeating 1715 Jacobite rising, English government tried to break up clan system in Highlands

12 Only one Parliament in Westminster attended by Scots MPs and lords

Investigations

bracket them together. How did you decide on the order?

4 Which of the reasons in the boxes would you say were the long-term causes of the Jacobite rebellion of 1745? Were there any short-term causes?

1 People supported the Jacobite Rising of 1745 for many reasons. These included religious, political, economic and personal reasons. Look at the reasons (1–12) set out above. Then group the reasons by placing the correct numbers in a copy of the table on the right.

2 Are there any other ways of dividing up (or grouping) the causes of the Jacobite Rising in 1745?

3 Which were the more important causes of the Jacobite Rising in 1745? Place the most important at the top of your list, and the least important at the bottom. If you think some of the causes are of equal importance,

	Numbers
Religious reasons for joining the Jacobite rising	
Political reasons for joining the Jacobite rising	
Economic reasons for joining the Jacobite rising	
Personal reasons for joining the Jacobite rising	

Source E   The battle of Culloden (1746)

Source F   The Duke of Cumberland is congratulated on the victory over the Scots

By *York corporation on*:
'... the late glorious success over rebellious savages.'
By *Edinburgh merchants on the defeat of*:
'...the barbarous inhabitants of the more remote parts of the country.'

Source G   The *Skye Boat Song* (traditional ballad)

S peed bonnie boat, like a bird on the wing
Onward, the sailors cry;
Carry the lad that's born to be king
Over the sea to Skye.
Burned are our homes; exile and death
Scatter the loyal men
Yet ere the sword cool in the sheath
Charlie will come again.

Following the defeat of the Jacobites at Culloden, there followed a campaign of terror by the British army against the Highland clans who had supported the rebellion. The wearing of Highland dress was banned, and the clans were forbidden to have weapons. By the mid-eighteenth century, a growing number of Scots accepted that their future was with Britain. Some Highlanders, as well as other Scots, went to start new lives in Britain's colonies overseas.

estigations

1 Identify the main features of the battle of Culloden by linking the letters and numbers in the picture in Source **E** with the correct descriptions in the chart on the right. The letters and numbers are done for you.

2 Write an account of the battle of Culloden: either as a war correspondent for a newspaper of the time, or as a letter from a defeated Jacobite to his sister.

3 What weapons are the Jacobites shown fighting with? What weapons are the Government troops shown using in the battle? Which side won the battle?

4 The caption of the painting reads 'View of the Glorious Victory obtained over the rebels'. What does this tell you about which side, English or Jacobite, the painting favours? Write a caption for the painting that would favour the Jacobites

5 Design a Wanted poster for capturing the Young Pretender, who had escaped following his defeat in battle at Culloden. Offer a reward of £30,000 for his capture.

Feature	Number
The Scottish town of Inverness	A
Jacobite army – about 5000 clansmen and cannon	B
Government army – about 9000 infantry, cavalry and cannon	C
Duke of Cumberland – leader of the government army	D
Events in battle	
Jacobites charging with broad swords and shields	1
Government muskets and cannon forcing Jacobites back	2
Jacobites attacking with broad swords and shields	3
Government bayonets and muskets forcing Jacobites back	4
Government cavalry attacking Jacobites left wing	5
Government cavalry attacking Jacobites from the rear	6

(Note: 2500 Jacobites were killed; 1500 more were killed in the pursuit; 1800 were taken prisoner.)

Kings and Parliament in the eighteenth century

Who were the Hanoverians?

When Queen Anne died in 1714, she left no heirs. Under the terms of the Act of Settlement (page 78) the throne then passed to George of Hanover, a Protestant German prince. He became George I (1714–27). During the eighteenth and nineteenth centuries, the descendants of George I ruled both Britain and the German state of Hanover.

Like the Tudor and Stuart monarchs before them, the Hanoverian kings still had power. The monarch could choose and dismiss his **ministers**. He could also create new lords. The members of the House of Lords were mostly wealthy landowners. They also used their wealth and power to control many of the seats in the House of Commons. The Hanoverian monarchs had to pay attention to Parliament and to the great lords who controlled it. The monarch could not rule without Parliament. The House of Commons had very important powers over taxation and finance. An Act of 1716 extended the life of Parliament from three to seven years. Each year the king and his ministers had to ask Parliament to agree to taxes.

How did the office of Prime Minister begin?

To help in governing the country, the monarch chose a group of men called ministers. After the 1688 Revolution, it became usual for the monarch to choose ministers from the political party, Whigs or Tories, that could control Parliament. This group of ministers became known as the **Cabinet**. At this time, the Cabinet usually met without the king being present. When the Cabinet met, it was **chaired** by the king's chief minister. After the meeting, this first or 'prime' minister told the king what the Cabinet had advised, and of any decisions they had made.

The title 'Prime Minister' began to be used in the eighteenth century. It was used to describe the most powerful minister in the government and in Parliament. From 1721–42 Sir Robert Walpole was the king's first or 'prime' minister. He is often referred to as Britain's first prime minister. Walpole led a powerful group of Whig politicians who were able to control Parliament.

How was the system of government in the eighteenth century different from that of today?

Under the Hanoverian monarchs the country gradually became a **constitutional monarchy** with a **parliamentary government**. However, Britain in the eighteenth century was far from being a democratic country. The monarch remained powerful. Parliament was controlled by the wealthy people who owned land and property. There were no proper political parties as we know them today. Very few people had the right to vote for members of the House of Commons. Only a few of the middle classes and none of the labouring classes were allowed to vote. No women were allowed to vote.

Source A Parliament in the mid eighteenth century

1 What scene is shown in Source **A**?

2 In this engraving of Parliament, can you find: King George II on the throne (1), leading nobles on the cloth of state (2), the large number of lords or nobles (3), the Speaker of the House of Commons (4), members of the House of Commons below the bar of the House (5)?

3 Compare Source **A** with the scene of Elizabeth I in Parliament (Source **A**, page 24). In the scene of 1584 only the monarch was allowed on the cloth of state. Which people are standing on the cloth of state in the scene of Parliament (1750) in Source **A**? What does this difference tell you about the changing power of the monarch?

4 Can you see any other features in the two scenes of Parliament which show the changing power of the monarch and Parliament between the sixteenth and eighteenth centuries?

5 What events and changes during the period 1500–1750 made Parliament more powerful and the monarch less powerful?

Key words

Ministers People in charge of running a government.

Cabinet The leading members of a country meeting together as a committee in a private room, known as a cabinet.

Chaired Acting as chairman of a committee.

Constitutional monarchy A monarchy whose powers are determined by law and custom. The constitution may be written down or, as in Britain, unwritten.

Parliamentary government In Britain the form of government that is made up of the monarch, the House of Lords and the House of Commons.

9 Everyday life
Population

What was family life like?

Between 1500 and 1750 the **population** of Britain grew from around 4.5 million to about 7 million. There were a number of reasons why the population grew slowly. These included bad harvests and diseases such as plague and small pox. A large number of children died in infancy or their early years. For example Queen Anne had twelve miscarriages, and six babies who had all died in early childhood. **Life expectancy** was short compared with the age that people often live to today. People were not expected to live long lives, although rich people usually lived longer than poor people.

What was women's place in society?

A woman's place in society depended upon the position of her father and, after she married, her husband. A woman was expected to obey the head of the family (father or husband). Women could not vote. They could not serve as **magistrates** but a few were **churchwardens**. Married women had no rights in law. What they owned became the property of their husband when they married. However, widows (women whose husbands had died) could own and do what they wanted with their own property.

Source A Family portrait of Lord Cobham, his wife, sister and children (Lord Cobham had an important position looking after England's sea defences and shipping)

Tudor dress

In Tudor times, rich ladies and gentlemen often wore clothes made of silk or velvet. These might be embroidered. Men wore jackets called doublets and long stockings called hose. Ladies used hooped frames, called farthingales, under their dresses to make them stand out. A ruff, a kind of large stiff collar worn around the neck, was fashionable for both men and women in Tudor times. Poor people and those who had to work with their hands such as labourers wore simple clothes. Women wore long skirts made of plain cloth.

1. See Source **A**. The Cobham family had this picture painted in 1567. How did Lord Cobham want his family to look in the portrait?

2. How does the painting show that the family was rich? In your own words, describe the people, their clothes, jewellery, food, tableware and pets.

3. The table is laid for dessert with grapes, cherries, peaches, apples, pears and nuts. Which fruits would be grown locally? Which would be imported from overseas?

4. How does the portrait show that Britain was involved in overseas trade and exploration?

5. Compare the painting with a modern family photograph (either your own or from a book or magazine). What differences can you see? Are there any similarities?

6. What would it be useful to know about the writer of Source **B** before using it as evidence?
   a) Did the writer believe that English married women were more free or less free than in some other European countries?
   b) What did the writer believe to be 'a Paradise'?

7. Was England 'a Paradise for married women'? Was it men or women who had power?

8. Whose permission was needed before a wife could behave in the way described?
   a) What does this tell you about the relations between wives and their husbands?
   b) Do you think all wives in England would agree with the writer?
   c) What does the writer tell you about the way some women spent their time?

9. **a)** To which class in society did the Cobham family belong (Source **A**)?
   b) Which two classes of society was the writer of Source **B** mainly describing? Which classes was he not describing?

Wives in England are ... in the power of their husbands, yet they are not kept so strictly as in Spain. Nor are they shut up ... . They go to market to buy what they like best to eat. They are well-dressed, fond of taking it easy and leave the care of the household to their stewards. They sit in front of their doors, dressed in fine clothes, to see and be seen by passers-by. ... All the rest of the time they spend in walking and riding, in playing at cards, in visiting their friends ... and childbirths and christenings. And all this with the permission of their husbands. This is why England is called the paradise of married women.

Source B 'England... the paradise of married women...', written by a Dutch visitor to London in 1575

Key words

Population The number of people living in a place or country.
Life expectancy The average number of years people can be expected to live.
Magistrates Officials allowed to try minor or less serious cases in court.
Churchwardens People who helped with the running of the affairs of a church or parish.

People and their place in society

How was society made up of different social classes?

At this time, people were very much aware of their place in society. There were many different **classes** of people. These ranged from nobles (lords) who were seen as the highest in the land down to labourers who were seen as the lowest class.

● Nobles (or lords) were seen as the highest **rank** in society next to the monarchy. Included in this class were dukes, earls, viscounts, and barons. These **hereditary** titles were handed down from father to eldest son. Nobles were wealthy and powerful. They led the army and navy in time of war. The highest ranks in the Church were archbishops and bishops.

● Gentry was the class below the nobles. They owned land which they rented out or paid people to farm for them. People belonging to the gentry included knights, squires and gentlemen. They often helped to keep law and order.

● Yeomen were farmers who owned small areas of land worth more than £2 a year. They had the right to vote in Parliamentary elections. Yeomen often helped in local government and served as jurors, constables and churchwardens.

● Merchants bought and sold goods. The richest merchants lived in London and other large ports where goods were imported and exported. Merchants often lived in large houses in the towns where they traded. They often bought land with the money they made. In this way, they and their children became part of the gentry class.

● Craftsmen made and sometimes sold goods. At a time when most goods were made by hand using craft tools, craftsmen and small traders played an important part in society, particularly in the towns. Many craftsmen benefited from the growth of towns and the increasing wealth of the country.

● Husbandmen did not usually own land. They rented land which they farmed as tenants.

● Labourers worked in the towns and in the countryside. They earned low wages. Those who worked on the land often lived in 'tied' cottages. This meant that the cottage went with the job. If the labourer lost his job, he lost his home as well. Labourers were seen as one of the lowest classes in society.

Investigations

1 Write a sentence about each of the people shown in Source **A** to explain how they earned their living.

2 **a)** Which of the crafts do you think would need most skill?
b) Which of the crafts do you think would be least skilful?

3 Write about three of the crafts and trades shown in Source **A**. Why were these craftsmen and traders more likely to live in the town than in the country?

4 What 'picture signs' might each hang outside their craft workshop? Draw the signs if you wish and include the tools being used and the products being made.

Key words

Classes Groups of people in society, graded usually by quality.
Rank A person's place in society or in the armed forces.
Hereditary Passed down from one generation to another.

The poor in town and country

There were large numbers of very poor people at this time. Some were unable to earn enough money to feed themselves and their families. They had to depend upon **charity** and **poor relief**. People who had no work and no money were called paupers. Some people, including ex-soldiers, gypsies and criminals moved about the country begging or stealing. They were called vagabonds.

Source A Whipping through the streets

How were the poor treated?

How poor people were treated depended very much on why they were poor. For example, those who had no work or were in need due to illness, **disability** or old age were allowed to beg in their own **parish** (that is the parish in which they were born). Those who were thought to be poor through their own fault were punished. A number of laws, known as **Poor Laws**, were passed by Parliament to deal with the problem of the poor.

What were the Poor Laws?

In 1572 an Act of Parliament was passed. This allowed parishes to charge local people a **poor rate** (a kind of local tax). The money from the poor rate could be used to build poorhouses and to provide help for those who were poor through no fault of their own. Poor children were to be **apprenticed**, that is they had to learn a trade. Those who were poor through laziness were to be punished. For example, beggars could be whipped, put in the stocks or branded with a hot iron.

Investigations

1 What name was given to those who moved about the country begging or stealing?

2 Can you find and describe the vagabond in Source **A**?
   a) How was the vagabond being punished?
   b) Why do you think the punishment was being carried out in public?
   c) Did the people watching seem to approve or disapprove of the whipping?

3 How did Parliament try to deal with the problem of having large numbers of poor people?

Key words

Charity Giving help, especially money, to those in need.
Poor relief Money given to poor people.
Disability Unable to do something.
Parish An area or district which has its own church and clergyman, and in which taxes were collected and the poor looked after.
Poor Laws Laws about giving help to poor people.
Poor rate A tax or sum of money which people had to pay to help the poor.
Apprenticed/apprentice A person learning a craft or trade.

The Poor Law Act of 1601

In 1601 an important Poor Law Act was passed. This brought together all the poor law acts that had been passed before. The Act gave local magistrates in each parish the power to charge a poor law rate. **Overseers of the poor** collected the rates. They also found work for poor people to do. Workhouses were built in many towns where poor people could work under supervision. The main aims of the Act of 1601 were to stop people being lazy and to keep the poor rate low. The Act remained in force until 1834.

Source B Giving out food to the poor of Tichbourne in Hampshire (1670)

Investigations

4 To which social class did Sir Henry Tichbourne and his family belong? Explain your answer.

5 a) What is being given out to the poor?
b) At which time of the year would the poor be most pleased to be given bread? Can you explain why?
c) This custom of giving to the poor was carried out each year and was hereditary. What did that mean?

6 Who do you think wanted the picture to be painted, and why?

7 a) How did the Tichbourne family want to be seen in the painting?

b) In what ways do the Tichbourne family and their friends look different from the poor tenants?

8 The onlookers included a black servant and a Quaker woman. Can you find and describe them?

9 How did the treatment given to the poor tenants in Tichbourne (Source **B**) differ from the treatment given to the vagabond (Source **A**)?

Key words

Overseers of the poor Parish officials whose job it was to give out the money to the poor.

Daily life

Most people in the countryside lived in houses built with a wooden framework. The spaces between the frame were filled in with wattle (sticks woven together) and daub (mud or clay). Houses were built using local materials because it was difficult and costly to carry stone, timber and bricks over long distances.

By Elizabethan times England had become a more peaceful place. Rich people no longer felt that they needed to live in castles and fortified homes to be safe. They began to build large houses, called mansions. These were built of brick and stone, sometimes in the shape of a letter E. The windows were made of a number of small panes of glass joined with strips of lead. Tall chimneys carried away the smoke from the large wood or coal fires. Kitchens had large fireplaces. Most food was cooked over a fire, on a roasting spit (a metal rod used to turn meat for roasting) or in a cauldron (a pot hanging on a chain). Furniture for all rooms was usually made of oak and was very heavy.

Source A Little Moreton Hall in Cheshire (built 1559–80)

Source B Half-timbered houses, by William Harrison writing in the 1570s

T he ancient manors and houses of our gentlemen are yet and for the most part of strong timber, in framing whereof our carpenters have been and are worthily preferred …

Investigations

1 Describe the home of the Moreton family (Source **A**). To which social class did they belong?

2 Can you say what kinds of materials were used to build Moreton Hall? Which kinds of skilled craftsmen would be employed in building the Hall?

Source C Montacute House

Source D Eighteenth-century peasant's cottage

3 Do you think that Montacute House was built for defence or for comfort? Is the house built mainly of timber, stone or brick?

4 **a)** Would Montacute House have been more or less costly to build than Moreton Hall?
b) Which of the two houses has most chimneys and windows?
c) Of the two types of houses, which do you think is the earliest in time?

5 Were the people who lived in the cottage (Source **D**) richer or poorer than the inhabitants of Little Moreton Hall and Montacute House?

6 **a)** Do you think it would be dark or light inside the cottage?
b) What kind of roof and chimneys did the cottage have?
c) What kind of fuel was used for the fire inside the cottage?

7 What kinds of material was the cottage built of? Were these expensive or cheap? Were they found locally or brought from a long distance?

8 In what ways might the cottage be unhealthy?

9 Would it take more time or less time to build than Little Moreton Hall (Source **A**)

10 Can you explain why there are fewer pictures of peasants' and labourers' cottages than of halls and great houses?

Investigations

Agriculture and the landscape

How did the wool and cloth trade affect farming?

Between 1500 and 1750 Britain was still mainly a farming country. Most people lived in the countryside and worked on the land. They grew crops and kept animals. Raw wool from sheep could be sold for a high price. This made many farmers want to keep more sheep. Thus more and more land began to be used for sheep farming. Sometimes, people who farmed the land also spun wool and wove cloth in their own homes. The wool trade, and the making of woollen cloth, helped to make the country more wealthy.

Source A   Sheep and shepherd

Enclosing the land

The joining together of strips of land to form fields enclosed by fences or stone walls, and the fencing of common land, is called enclosure. In the period between 1500 and 1750 enclosure of land to form larger farms increased. This meant that land could be farmed more efficiently. At this time too, some areas of woodland were cleared and many marshes were drained. These changes provided more land for farming.

How was enclosure carried out?

Sometimes enclosure was carried out with the agreement of those who farmed and used the land. At other times, wealthy landowners enclosed the land by force. This sometimes resulted in people losing their homes and their jobs. Some people were

against these changes and there were protests against enclosure in 1536, 1569 and 1607.

Source B   Sir Thomas More in his book *Utopia* comments on enclosure

> S heep ... eat up and swallow ... men themselves ... noblemen and gentlemen ... and certain abbots ... leave no ground for tillage, they enclose all into pastures: they throw down houses ... pluck down towns and leave nothing standing, but only the church to be made into a sheephouse ... the husbandmen be thrust out of their own ... they must needs depart away ... and soon what remains for them but to steal, and be hung ... or wander about and beg?

Investigations

1 a) Why was the wool trade and the making of woollen cloth important for England?
  b) What effect did sheep farming have on the way land was used?

2 What were the reasons for the enclosure of land?

3 Did it cost a lot of money to keep sheep? Did their wool bring in much money to the farmer and

landowner? Does the shepherd employed by the farmer and landowner look wealthy or poor (Source **A**)?

4 Why was Sir Thomas More (Source **B**) against the enclosure of land for sheep-farming? Can you explain how the sheep had 'eat up and swallow ... men themselves ...'?

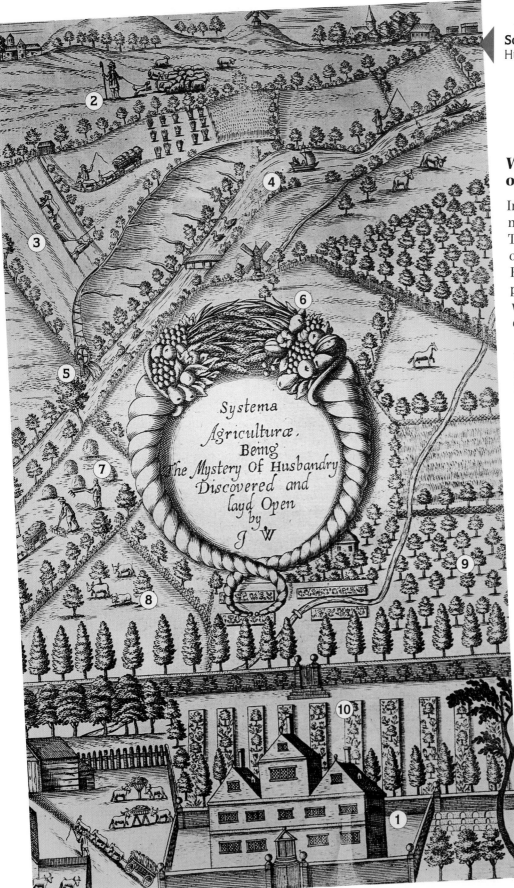

Systema
Agriculturæ,
Being
The Mystery Of Husbandry
Discovered and
layd Open
by
J W

What were the results of changes in farming?

In the eighteenth century more enclosure took place. This was sometimes carried out by local agreement. However, increasingly, private Acts of Parliament were used to carry out enclosure.

The changes in farming the land increased the amount of food that could be produced. This meant that many landowners and farmers grew rich. However, the new ways meant that some farm labourers were without work. Some were turned off the land. Many were no longer allowed to graze their animals on the commons or gather wood for their fires. Life became harder for many poor families.

Source D Farming scene in the mid eighteenth century

5 The picture in Source **C** is from a book written in 1676. It shows what a well-run landed estate should be like. Identify the main features of the picture by

linking the numbers in the picture with the correct descriptions in the chart on the left. The first one is done for you.

Feature	Number
Landowner's house set within walled courtyard	1
A well laid-out garden	
An orchard for fruit	
Cattle grazing	
A hay meadow	
A water mill	
A navigable river used by small boats	
Field being ploughed for growing crops	
A windmill for grinding corn	
Shepherd and sheep in the pasture	
Describe a day spent with the landowner on his estate (Source **C**)	

6 Two horns of plenty (called 'cornucopiae') filled with farming produce are shown at the centre of the picture. Can you explain the link between the two cornucopiae and the way the farm was run?

7 How many people are working on the farm in Source **D**? List all their activities, for example – maid fetching water. In what ways are the children and young people employed?

8 How do you know that the family probably earned part of their living from making cloth as well as from farming?

9 a) How and why did changes take place in farming?
 b) What were the benefits and the disadvantages of the farming changes?

10 How would a day spent with the farmer in Source **D** be different from the day you have described for Source **C**?

Industry

How was the making of woollen cloth organised?

In the period between 1500 and 1750 many goods were made in people's own homes. This is known as **cottage industry**. Goods made in this way included shoes and other leather items, pottery and woollen cloth. Sometimes, especially in the woollen industry, a merchant might rent out raw materials and tools to cottage workers, so that they could make goods in their own homes. In the towns there were many different kinds of traders and craftsmen.

The woollen industry

Next to farming, the woollen industry was the most important occupation. It was protected by many Acts of Parliament. For example, one Act said that the dead had to be buried in woollen cloth. Another Act banned the export of raw wool and machines which could be used to make cloth.

Spinning and **weaving** were carried out in people's own homes in the countryside or small villages. The finishing stages of making cloth, for example **fulling**, **dyeing** and **bleaching**, were carried out in the towns. Cloth was also taken to the towns to be sold.

In some areas, the making of woollen cloth was organised by rich merchants. In East Anglia, for example, merchants brought raw wool from Lincolnshire and Leicestershire and gave it to workers to make cloth in their own homes. Usually the whole family helped to make the cloth. For example, children might **card** or **comb** the wool to free it of tangles, women might spin the wool into **yarn**, and the yarn would be woven into cloth by the men. When the cloth was ready, the merchant took it to sell in the towns and made his **profit**.

In the West Country (Devon) high quality woollen cloth was made. Cheaper kinds of cloth were made in the West Riding of Yorkshire by workers who usually owned their own **spinning wheels** and **weaving looms**. In Ireland and Scotland flax was grown for the making of linen.

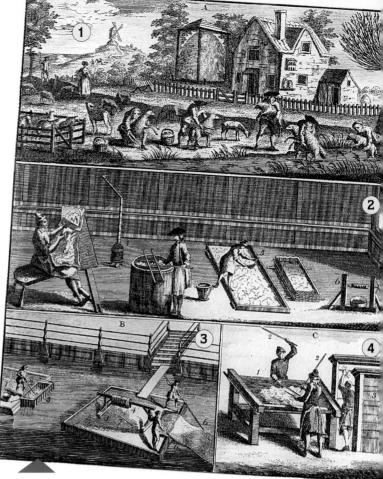

Source A The Preparation of Wool (*c.*1700)

Source B Women workers in the linen industry in Ireland

The coal industry

In the sixteenth century most coal was taken from the ground by surface mining or digging shallow pits. Gradually, pits became deeper and by the seventeenth century there was a problem of water collecting in the deeper mines. By 1750 **engines** were being used to pump out the water in some mines. The most important engines were those

invented by Thomas Savery in 1698 and by Thomas Newcomen in 1712. On the larger coalfields, **waggonways** and horse-drawn waggons were used to carry the coal to the **navigable** rivers.

The Durham and Northumberland coalfield was the most important at this time. From this coalfield, coal was sent to London by sea. Coal was used in some homes for heating and cooking. By the early eighteenth century some industries were using coal. These included the brewing, soapmaking, and sugar refining industries. The salt, pottery, brick, nail and glass-making industries also began to use some coal. This growing demand increased the importance of the coal industry.

The iron industry

There had been an iron industry in Britain for many centuries but it had grown only slowly. The raw material for the iron industry was iron ore, a rock obtained from the ground. Until the eighteenth century the main fuel used in the making of iron was charcoal. Charcoal was made by burning wood. The trees used to make charcoal became scarce. The **ironmasters** had to move their ironworks from the old iron-making centres such as the Weald of Sussex and Kent. They moved to parts of the country where woods were more plentiful. The new areas for the iron industry included Scotland, South Wales, Shropshire and South Yorkshire.

Key words

Cottage industry   Making things or running a business from the home.
Spinning   Making yarn or thread from raw material e.g. wool, cotton, silk.
Weaving   To make cloth by crossing thread (called warp and weft) in and out.
Fulling   Cleaning and thickening cloth.
Dyeing   Changing the colour by using dye.
Bleaching   To whiten or lighten with sunlight or chemicals.
Card   Using a wire brush to untangle fibres before spinning into thread.
Comb   To separate and cleanse woollen fibres using a tool known as a comb.
Yarn   Spun thread.
Profit   Getting more money back than has been laid out.
Spinning wheels   Machines for spinning raw material, such as wool or cotton, into thread.
Weaving looms   Machines for weaving thread into cloth.
Engines   Mechanical parts working together, usually to provide power or movement.
Waggonways   Rails along which waggons were pulled, especially to carry coal.
Navigable   Ships and boats able to pass along.
Ironmasters   People who manufacture (make) iron goods.

Investigations

1 Each of the four scenes in the preparation of wool has been given a number. Select the correct number to fit the following descriptions:

Description	Correct number
Sheep being sheared of fleece	
The wool being combed out	
The wool being worked	
The wool being beaten before being spun	

2 How do you know that Parliament was interested in protecting the woollen industry?

3 Source **B** shows Protestant settlers from Scotland working in the linen industry in Ireland. Write one paragraph describing the work being carried out by the women.

4 Describe the Newcomen engine (Source **C**). What was the engine used for?

Travel and transport

▶ **How was transport improved?**

Carrying goods by water, especially bulky goods such as coal, was easier and cheaper than using the roads. Therefore, many rivers were important for **inland navigation**. These covered much of the country and few places were more than thirty miles from navigable rivers. From the later seventeenth century onwards, many rivers were deepened and straightened. This increased the stretches of rivers that were navigable. As a result, a growing number of towns became inland ports. Examples include Leeds, Derby and Bath. By 1750 there were over 1000 miles of navigable waterways in the country.

Source A
Carrying coal to Cambridge by water

Transport by land

Most people travelled on foot or on horseback. Some people and some goods were carried on carts which had broad wheels. By the eighteenth century, rich people often travelled in their own coaches. These often had seats and curtains.

● Stage coaches were used from the late seventeenth century onwards. These could travel about thirty or forty miles in a day. They stopped at inns along the route. A journey by stage coach between London and Edinburgh, for example, took eight or nine days.

● The post chaise was another means of travel. This light and covered carriage was pulled by two, or sometimes four, horses. When the horses grew tired they could be changed for fresh horses along the route. This meant that the coach could travel more quickly.

● The post horse was the fastest way to travel. It could be hired from government postmasters along the route and could cover about ten miles in an hour. Post horses were used to carry the mail.

How did the postal service develop?

In the early seventeenth century, the main purpose of the Post Office was to carry royal letters. Later, members of the public were also allowed to use the postal service. However, the service was badly run. Letters often went missing and the service was slow. In 1720 Ralph Allen of Bath paid an annual rental of £2000 to the government for the right to develop a postal system which linked all parts of the country.

Key words

Inland navigation Communication by rivers and canals.
Turnpike trustees People with the duty or legal power to administer the money raised and used for turnpike roads.
Turnpike roads Roads on which a toll was charged for vehicles to be used.
Tolls Charges for passing along a road or over a bridge.
Interest Money paid for the use of money lent.

How were the roads improved?

Many roads were in a bad state of repair. Each parish was responsible for the upkeep of roads in its area. However, as the amount of traffic increased, a better system of repairing the roads was needed. From the late seventeenth century onwards turnpike trusts were set up to improve some roads.

Acts of Parliament were passed to allow groups of local people, known as **turnpike trustees**, to improve roads. These roads were known as **turnpike roads**. Before 1750 most turnpike roads were around London and in the south-east of England. **Tolls** were charged for traffic using the turnpike roads. The money raised from charging tolls was used to repair the road and to pay **interest** to the trustees.

estigations

1 Source **A** shows the river Cam and one of the colleges at Cambridge University. Count the number of chimneys you can see. Explain the connection between the number of chimneys and the coal being carried on the river.

2 Why would a College need much coal? What other goods might be brought in by water?

3 The boats carrying coal are joined together. How did this increase the amount of coal carried? Why was coal carried by water rather than by road?

4 **a)** For what other purpose was the river used?
   b) How were passengers sheltered when being carried along or across the river?

5 List the different ways in which goods and people are shown being carried in Source **B**. Are there any forms of transport used in the eighteenth century which are not shown in the picture?

6 What animals can you see in the picture? Why were horses important for travel and transport at this time? What other uses did they have?

7 All the buildings in the picture had been built after 1666. Can you say why (page 71 may help you)?

8 Can you name the world famous domed church visible in the distance? Who built it? When and why was it built (see page 71)?

9 List the similarities and differences between the scene in Cornhill in 1750 and a modern street scene.

10 How were roads improved and repaired in the eighteenth century?

Trade

As well as trading with
countries in Europe,
Britain began to find new
overseas markets much
further away. As explorers
discovered new lands and
peoples, the growth in
trade, both **imports** and
exports increased. A
number of important trading companies were set up
in the sixteenth century. The Muscovy Company, set
up in 1555 aimed to increase trade with Russia. In
1581, the Levant Company was granted a
monopoly of trade with countries in the eastern
Mediterranean. This meant that the Company was
the only English company trading to that part of the
world. Trade with India began in Elizabethan times.
In 1600 the East India Company was set up to trade
with countries in the Indian Ocean and the Far
East. Silk, **calico**, cotton and **gold bullion** were
imported into the country. New kinds of food were
brought into the country. These included coffee, tea,
potatoes and tomatoes.

From the mid sixteenth century onwards,
Britain traded in black slaves. This trade in human
beings greatly harmed the black peoples of Africa.
The trade brought great wealth to English traders
and shippers. In the eighteenth century Britain had
the right to supply slaves to Spain's empire in the
Americas. This increased the profits from the slave
trade, and ports such as Bristol, Liverpool and
Glasgow grew rich. Sugar and tobacco were brought

Source A A London
coffee house

from the West Indies. By 1750
Glasgow had become Britain's
biggest trading port for tobacco. Large amounts of
sugar and rum were also traded through Glasgow.

By the eighteenth century, Britain was
becoming the most important trading country in
Europe. Her empire, at this time, included 13
colonies in North America, and colonies in Canada
and the West Indies.

Banking

The growth of trade led to the development of
banks. Also, in the late seventeenth century, the
government needed large amounts of money to fight
the wars against France. These needs led to
important changes in banking. In 1694 an Act of
Parliament set up the Bank of England. It became
the most important centre for **finance** in the world.
The English pound sterling became the strongest
(the most valuable) **currency** in Europe.

Key words

Trade Buying and selling goods.
Imports Goods brought into a country.
Exports Goods sent out of a country.
Monopoly The sole or single right of dealing in
something.
Calico Cotton cloth often plain white or
unbleached.
Gold bullion Gold in bulk (large amount) before
being made into coin, etc.
Finance The management of money.
Currency The money used in a country.

Investigations

1 Why do you think coffee houses, such as that
shown in Source **A**, became popular meeting places?
  a) Why would merchants and bankers find a coffee
house useful?
  b) What kinds of things might members of
Parliament talk about in a coffee house?

2 Some of the customers in the coffee house are
reading. What do you think they are reading?

3 How many coffee pots can you see? How was the
coffee kept hot?

The growth of towns

London was the **capital** city. Its population grew from about 50,000 in 1520 to about 675,000 in 1750. It became the biggest city in the world and was an important political, social and trading centre. Goods were brought into London from all parts of the country and from many parts of the world. Growing trade increased the wealth of the city, and many fine buildings were built. However, the growing population in London meant that some areas of the city became overcrowded. Houses were often built upwards instead of outwards to save space. Many streets were narrow and dirty.

Other towns such as Norwich, Bristol and York and, later, Liverpool, Manchester and Birmingham also grew in size. By 1750 more and more people were living in towns. These had become centres of trade where goods were made, bought and sold. Farmers brought corn, cattle, poultry, vegetables, fruit, butter, cheese and honey to markets in the towns to sell.

Source A   Celia Fiennes visits Bristol (1698)

> This town is a very great tradeing citty ... the largest next London; the river Avon ... beares shipps and barges up to the key (quay), where I saw the harbour was full of shipps ...the streetes are ... preserved by their useing sleds to carry all things about ...

Source B   The dockside quay at Bristol in the eighteenth century

---

Investigations

1 Using Sources **A** and **B** and the following information, write a paragraph to describe a dockside quay: *sailing ships loading or unloading goods, *small cranes on the dock quay to help move goods, *moving goods with horses and sledges.

2 Can you see in the picture (Source **B**) the sleds described by Celia Fiennes in Source **A**? Why were they used?

3 Why was Bristol growing rapidly in the late seventeenth and eighteenth centuries?

4 How do the ships shown in Source **B** differ from the boats on the river Cam (Source **A**, page 96)? Can you explain the differences?

Key words

Capital   The most important town or city in a country or region.

10 The arts and sciences

Depth Study: The Renaissance

- **What do we mean by the arts?**
- **What do we mean by Renaissance art?**

When we talk about the arts we mean painting, architecture, music and literature (stories, plays and poetry). We also mean the performing arts such as drama and dancing. During the period covered in this book these arts were influenced by changes and ideas which affected all countries in Europe. It led to new ways of presenting some of the arts. The word **Renaissance** is used to describe these ways.

The word Renaissance means re-birth. The artists, writers and musicians of this period became interested in the **culture** of ancient Greece and Rome. The Renaissance began in Italy and slowly spread throughout Europe. It was at its most popular in the sixteenth century. The ideas of the Renaissance were slow to reach Britain. They came here mainly from France, Flanders (modern Belgium) and Germany.

Painting

The ideas of the Renaissance in painting were brought to England by the German portrait painter Hans Holbein the Younger (1497–1543). Holbein came to live in London in the 1530s. He worked at the royal court of King Henry VIII. He painted portraits of the king and of courtiers.

By the 1540s, following Henry VIII's break with Rome and the dissolution of the monasteries (Chapter 4), paintings showing religious scenes had become less popular. There was more interest in showing the importance of the family, people and their lifestyles. Above all, the painting of portraits became popular. These were mostly of monarchs, nobles and gentry.

Royal portraits were sometimes painted for political reasons. For example, the 'Armada portrait' of Elizabeth I (page 23) gives the view that God sent a great storm to destroy the Spanish Armada and to help England and the Queen. Miniatures (small

portraits) were also popular. Nicholas Hilliard, an Elizabethan artist, was very skilled in painting miniatures.

Later, portraits giving a favourable view of Charles I, his queen Henrietta Maria, and members of his court were painted by Sir Anthony Van Dyck (1599–1641). Van Dyck had come from Flanders (modern Belgium) to settle in England in the 1630s.

Source A   Henry VIII painted by Hans Holbein

Source B
Charles I painted by Van Dyck

1 Look at the portrait of Henry VIII (Source **A**) and write down three words which you think best describes the king. Write down three words which you think best describe Charles I (Source **B**). Are any of the words you have used the same for both portraits?

2 Why and how might a monarch want a portrait to show his or her power?

3 In trying to show the power of a king or queen, which of the following might an artist consider important: the face and the figure of the monarch; the pose; the clothes; the objects to be included in the picture? Can you list these in order of importance?

4 The portrait of Charles I (Source **B**) showed the king as he might have wished to be remembered in history.

Select three of the following words which you think best describe Charles in his portrait: elegant, authority, cultured, gentlemanly, fashionable, strong, powerful.

5 What objects might a monarch want included in his or her portrait, and why?

6 Why might courtiers and noblemen try to copy the fashions shown in royal portraits?

Key words

Renaissance Revival of interest in ancient Greek and Roman art and literature. A re-birth of the arts and literature of ancient Rome and Greece, popular in Europe from the fourteenth to sixteenth centuries.
Culture The arts and customs of a country at a particular time.

Architecture

In England an architect called Inigo Jones (1573–1652) began to use the ideas of the Italian Renaissance in his buildings. He built the Banqueting House in Whitehall, London. The ceiling of the Banqueting House was painted by a famous Flemish artist called Rubens.

Later, a number of architects copied the style of an Italian architect called Palladio. Palladio based his ideas on the buildings of ancient Rome. Many great houses in Britain were built to look like the villas in Italy. This style of building is sometimes called Palladian.

In the later seventeenth century the famous architect and scientist Sir Christopher Wren (1632–1723) used some of the ideas of the Renaissance in his work He designed and rebuilt St Paul's Cathedral and fifty other churches in London which had been destroyed in the Great Fire (page 71).

Source C Ceiling at the Banqueting House in Whitehall

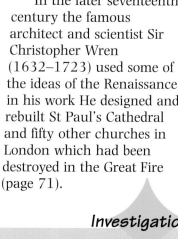

Investigations

1 Who built the Banqueting House? Who painted the ceiling (Source **C**)?

2 The painted ceiling shows King James I swapping his earthly crown for a heavenly one. How does this show that the Stuart kings believed in divine right? What was the divine right of kings (page 45)?

3 Holbein (Source **A**), Van Dyck (Source **B**) and Rubens (Source **C**) were invited from mainland Europe to paint in England. What does this suggest about English painting? What does it suggest about European painting?

4 The works of art shown in Sources **A**, **B** and **C** were ordered by monarchs. This shows that the monarchs were patrons of art. What is a patron?

5 Why was it important for an artist to have a patron? Give as many reasons as you can.

6 Who was executed outside the Banqueting House in 1649 (page 54)?

Source D Courtiers and nobility dancing in Elizabethan times

Music

There were many different kinds of music at this time. Travelling minstrels sang and played music in the towns, villages and the houses of the wealthy. Very rich people sometimes had their own musicians. They might play to entertain them during meals and sometimes for dancing. Elizabeth I, for example, loved dancing. Ordinary people danced in the open air and around the village Maypole. Morris dancing (a kind of folk dancing) was also popular.

Madrigals were very popular during the reign of Elizabeth I and James I. Madrigals were songs performed by four to six people, usually without musical instruments. Famous composers and writers of madrigals include William Byrd (1543–1623) and Thomas Morley (1557–1602).

Two famous composers of the late seventeenth and early eighteenth centuries were Henry Purcell and George Frederick Handel. Henry Purcell (1659–95) composed opera. He also wrote religious music. George Frederick Handel (1685–1759) was born in Germany. He came to live in England and became a favourite of King George I. Handel composed music for the organ. He also wrote operas and is famous for his oratorios (an oratorio is music written for solo singers, chorus and orchestra using the words of the Bible). In 1742 Handel wrote his best known oratorio called *Messiah*.

Source E Village festivities

Investigations

1 What activities are shown taking place in Sources **D** and **E**?

2 Which class of people are shown dancing in Source **D**? Which class of people are shown in Source **E**? How does the dancing shown in Source **D** differ from that shown in Source **E**?

3 Look at the following list, and decide to which of the Sources (**D** or **E**) each belong: **a)** stringed instruments, **b)** playing the pipes, **c)** drinking beer, **d)** ruffs, **e)** dancing in a ring, **f)** silk dresses.

4 It has been suggested that Queen Elizabeth I is shown in this painting (Source **D**). If true, which figure do you think is that of Elizabeth? What evidence suggests that the painting might include Elizabeth?

5 If you could attend and take part in ONE of the entertainments shown (Source **D** or **E**) which would you choose, and why? Write a description of the entertainment you have chosen to attend.

Literature

The first printing press in England was set up at Westminster by William Caxton in 1476. The printing press made it cheaper to print books. It became easier to spread knowledge, including the ideas of the Renaissance. In 1516, an English scholar called Thomas More (1478–1535) wrote a book called *Utopia*, which was first published in Flanders. In the book, More imagined a happy world, an island, where property, money and war had no place. The book was also against enclosure of the land which it was believed might lead to unemployment (page 91).

Source F Illustration from Thomas More's *Utopia* written in 1516

Source G William Shakespeare

Mr. WILLIAM
SHAKESPEARES
COMEDIES,
HISTORIES, &
TRAGEDIES.
Published according to the True Originall Copies.

Drama

Actors often travelled about the country. They performed in the streets or inn yards of towns. In 1576 the first playhouse, called the 'Theatre' was built in London by James Burbage. In 1596 Burbage also opened the 'Blackfriars', the first covered theatre in London. His son, Cuthbert Burbage built a famous theatre called the 'Globe' in 1599. This octagonal (eight-sided) theatre was open to the sky. Theatres were a popular form of entertainment for all classes of people. Many people came to the Globe to see the plays of William Shakespeare.

1592 First mentioned as a dramatist, writing in London

1601 Death of his father, John Shakespeare

1564 Born in Stratford, son of John Shakespeare (a glover) and Mary (née Arden)

1582 Marries Anne Hathaway

1596 Death of son Hamnet

1608 Birth of William Shakespeare's granddaughter Elizabeth

1616 Shakespeare returns to Stratford

1623 Publication of *First Folio* – the earliest collection of Shakespeare's works

1560 1570 1580 1590 1600 1610 1620 1630

1583 Birth of daughter Susanna

1595 Wrote *Romeo and Juliet*

1607 Marriage of daughter Susanna to John Hall

1610 Shakespeare returns to Stratford

1585 Birth of twins Hamnet and Judith

1597 Shakespeare buys large house in Stratford, called "New Place"

Source H The Globe Theatre in London

The Globe

Who was William Shakespeare?

William Shakespeare was England's greatest writer of plays and poetry. He was born in Stratford upon Avon in 1564 and died there in 1616. He moved to London in 1594 as an actor and writer of plays. This was the time when the Renaissance was at its height in England. Shakespeare wrote 38 plays and many poems and sonnets (a poem of fourteen lines). His plays are still acted today all over the world. He is probably the world's most famous playwright.

Investigations

1 When did Thomas More write his book *Utopia*? Using the text and the information in Source **F** say what Thomas More's *Utopia* was like

2 The word 'utopia' comes from the Greek word meaning 'no where' or 'no place'. Did the utopia described by Thomas More really exist?

3 What happened to Thomas More in 1535 and why (page 29)?

4 What would your own 'utopia' be like?

5 What developments made it easier to produce books such as *Utopia*? How did this help to spread knowledge and new ideas?

6 Who was William Shakespeare and why is he famous today? Draw a family tree of the Shakespeare family.

7 Use the lifeline and family tree to answer the following questions:
• how old was William Shakespeare when he got married? • how many children did William and Anne have? • where did William spend most of his life betwen 1592 and 1610? • how old was he when the Globe theatre was opened? • how old was he when his granddaughter Elizabeth was born? • how old was William when he died?

8 Look at Source **G**, and say how Shakespeare's plays were grouped. Can you explain what each of the three groups were about? Can you give an example of one play for each group?

9 a) What London building is shown in Source **H** and what was it used for?
b) What other theatres were built in London at this time?
c) What does the building of many theatres in London in the time of Elizabeth I suggest about entertainment?

Leisure

Source A Hunting and hawking in Elizabethan times

In the period 1500 to 1750 a growing number of new sports and entertainments were played. These were in addition to the traditional sports that people had long enjoyed. Such activities were an important part of everyday life. In 1618, for example, in a book called *The Book of Sports*, King James I supported the right of people to play. However, during the period of the Interregnum, from 1649 to 1660, many sporting activities and theatrical entertainments were banned (page 60). After the Restoration of the monarchy in 1660 many sporting activities and entertainments were allowed again. They continued to grow in popularity.

What were the main sporting activities in the period 1500 to 1750?

- Jousting was an activity in which two horsemen charged at each other with a lance. Each hoped to unseat the other. Jousting could be a dangerous sport. It was enjoyed by the nobility and was very popular during the early part of Henry VIII's reign.
- Tilting was a sporting activity in which a lance was used to try to spear small metal rings. It was popular at tournaments.
- Tournaments were contests to show off fighting skills, using blunted weapons. They were often held to entertain the royal court. In the later Elizabethan period, for example, tournaments were held to celebrate the anniversary of Elizabeth I becoming queen.
- Hunting and fishing were enjoyed for the sport and for the food it provided. Hunting, with dogs or hawks, was a popular sport for monarchs, the nobility and the gentry. The hunting of wild animals included deer and foxes. They were hunted partly to control the numbers but mainly for sport. From the

seventeenth century onwards, most hunting took place in the game parks and large estates of wealthy landowners. Hawking (hunting with a bird of prey) was also a favourite sport for the wealthy. At this time, fishing was becoming more popular. *The Compleat Angler* by Izaak Walton was published in 1653.

- Horse racing became more popular in the seventeenth and eighteenth centuries. The Stuart kings were great supporters of horse-racing. At first, races were held between the horses owned by the nobility and gentry. Soon larger meetings were being held with prizes of silver cups and plates being awarded to the winners. By the eighteenth century many towns were holding race meetings, including Epsom and Newmarket.
- Cockfighting involved the placing of bets on these birds before putting them in a pit to fight each other. By the eighteenth century it had become a very popular gambling activity.

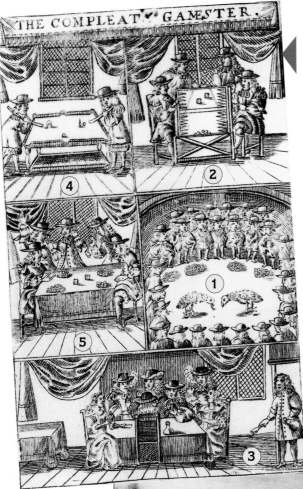

THE COMPLEAT GAMESTER.

Source B Illustration from *The Compleat Gamester* published in 1674

B illiards from Spain at first derived its name,
   Both an ingenious, and a cleanly game.
Now t'Irish, or Back-Gammoners we come,
Who wish their money, with their men safe home.

Next here are Hazzards played the other way,
By box and dice; tis Hazzard is the play.
After these three the Cock-pit claims a name;
A sport gentile, and called a Royal Game.

Now see the gallants crowd about the pit,
And most are stocked with money more than wit;
Else sure they would not, with so great a stir,
Lay ten to one on a cock's faithless spur.

Lastly, observe the women with what grace
They sit, and look their partners in the face.
The women knew their game, then cry'd, enough,
Let's leave off Whist, and go to Putt, or Ruff.

Source C *Entertainments*

Games such as bowls, tennis, hockey, football and cricket were played by all kinds of people. However, they were often different to the games as we know them today. For example, real tennis was very different to the modern game, and football was sometimes played with the whole village taking part.

Source D A Cricket Match in 1743

estigations

1 What sporting activity is shown in Source **A**?

2 Are the hunters rich or poor? How can you tell?

3 What other sporting activities did people enjoy in Elizabethan times? Which would be enjoyed mainly by the wealthy? Which might be enjoyed by the poor?

4 Which of these sports might be said to be cruel? Can you say why?

5 Each of the activities in the illustration (Source **B**) has been numbered. Match the numbers with the descriptions of the games in the verses (Source **C**).

6 Why did games become more popular after 1660 (page 63)?

7 a) Which of the games or pastimes popular in the seventeenth century are not common today?
b) Which games and pastimes popular today were not known in the seventeenth century?
c) Which games or pastimes popular in the seventeenth century are still played today?

8 What game is being played in Source **D**? Would you say that this game was being played by village people or nobles?

9 What differences can you see between the game of cricket played in 1743 and the modern game of today? Are there any similarities?

Schools and universities

How did schools change?

Schooling was mainly for those who could afford to pay for it. It was available for boys much more than for girls. Many grammar schools were started in the Tudor period. These usually charged a fee but had some free places for the clever sons of poorer families. Discipline was strict and pupils were often beaten. Most were taught the classics, that is Latin and Greek. In the sixteenth century, the teaching of writing became important, and from the seventeenth century onwards, more subjects were taught, including English and mathematics.

By the eighteenth century there was a wide range of schools providing education. In addition to the grammar and public schools, which were mainly for the wealthy and the middle classes, a growing number of private schools provided education for older children, mainly boys. Parish and dame schools were mainly for the children of poorer families. The charity schools also provided education for the poor.

At Oxford and Cambridge universities many new colleges were founded. A growing number of the sons of the gentry class spent some time at University. They might also attend the Inns of Court in London where they studied law. Scotland had more Universities than England at this time.

The Grand Tour

The young sons of noble and gentry families often went on a tour of Europe. This 'grand tour' as it was known was undertaken as part of a young person's education. Young people travelled abroad, perhaps for one or two years. They had a servant to look after them and a tutor to help with their studies. It was expected that the tour would help them to learn languages. It was also to develop good manners and to learn about the arts and way of life of other peoples. They often met many dangers on their travels including bad roads, uncomfortable inns, strange food and disease. Their route across Europe passed through Holland, Flanders and on to Italy. The Grand Tour meant that, in some ways, the young noblemen of Europe shared in a common culture.

Investigations

1 Describe the room and all the things you can see taking place in Source **A**. How can you tell that it is a schoolroom? What evidence is there that the scholars were beaten?

2 At least three different subjects were being taught in the Tudor schoolroom. Can you name them?

3 Were the scholars boys or girls? How many people can be seen teaching the scholars? Were they men or women?

4 Why were the pupils lining up? What might happen if they made a mistake in reading?

5 How is this schoolroom different from your own classroom today? Are there any similarities?

A scientific age

When we talk about the sciences we mean looking at, finding out about, and explaining the world we live in. During the period 1500 to 1750 great advances were made in scientific knowledge. New discoveries were made and important experiments were carried out.

Medicine

In the sixteenth century, people had very little knowledge of medicine or how the body worked. Doctors often had little or no training. They suggested 'bleeding' patients as a treatment for many illnesses. In 1628 a doctor called William Harvey (1578–1657) worked out how the blood moves around the body. This is called **circulation**. He drew pictures to record and explain his discoveries. Harvey was a doctor at the royal court, and looked after the Stuart monarchs James I and Charles I.

Alchemy

Alchemy, the practice of trying to turn cheap metals into gold, had been studied for centuries. It was based on the idea of all matter being able to change. Many scientists, including Isaac Newton, had an interest in alchemy. The study of alchemy helped in the development of chemistry.

Source A
William Harvey talking about his ideas to King Charles I

Source B
Alchemists at work

Circulation
The movement of blood around the body from and to the heart.

Key words

Investigations

1 Can you find and describe King Charles I and William Harvey in Source **A**?

2 **a)** What do you think Harvey is explaining to the king?
b) Which part of the deer is Harvey removing to show the king?
c) Why would Harvey want to dissect (cut up) an animal in this way?

3 How might such experiments be useful in the advance of medicine and surgery? What was Harvey's most important discovery?

4 What are the alchemists shown trying to do in Source **B**? Write a short description of the scene in the workshop explaining what alchemy is.

5 How did the alchemists try to change lead, iron and other metals into gold? How do metals change when they are heated? Do they become different metals? Why were alchemists unsuccessful?

6 Why did alchemists often work in secret? What secrets did they hope to discover? What secrets did they fear others might steal from them?

Science in Britain

Some of Britain's greatest scientists lived in the seventeenth century. Francis Bacon (1561–1626) wrote a book about scientific ways of finding out about the world. It was called *The New Atlantis* (1626). Robert Boyle (1627–91) made exciting discoveries in chemistry. He is best known for his experiments using the air pump. A scientist called Robert Hooke was an early inventor of a microscope which helped scientists to look at objects which could not easily be seen with the human eye.

A scientist called Isaac Newton (1642–1727) built a new kind of telescope. This reflecting telescope used a mirror instead of a lens to study the planets, moon and stars. Newton also carried out experiments with light. By using a prism he discovered that white light is made up of many colours (an example of this is the rainbow). Newton wrote a famous book on mathematics called *Principia*. He also explained the laws of motion and how gravity works. Newton was a professor at Cambridge University and, later, President of the Royal Society.

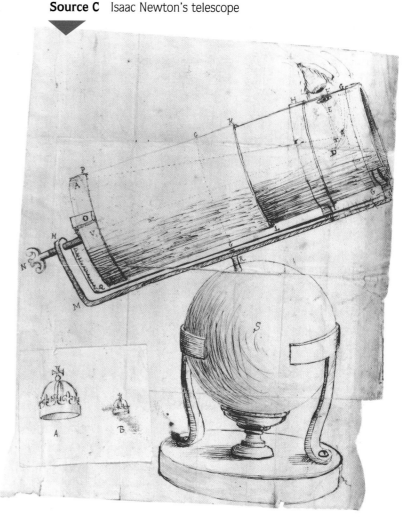

Source C Isaac Newton's telescope

Lifeline: Isaac Newton

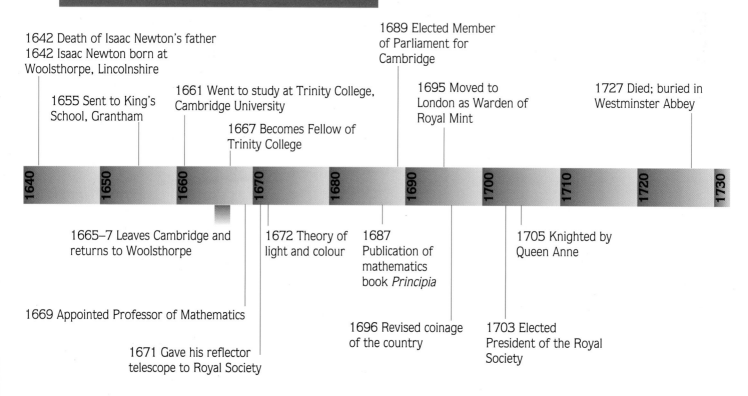

1642 Death of Isaac Newton's father
1642 Isaac Newton born at Woolsthorpe, Lincolnshire

1655 Sent to King's School, Grantham

1661 Went to study at Trinity College, Cambridge University

1667 Becomes Fellow of Trinity College

1689 Elected Member of Parliament for Cambridge

1695 Moved to London as Warden of Royal Mint

1727 Died; buried in Westminster Abbey

1640 1650 1660 1670 1680 1690 1700 1710 1720 1730

1665–7 Leaves Cambridge and returns to Woolsthorpe

1672 Theory of light and colour

1687 Publication of mathematics book *Principia*

1705 Knighted by Queen Anne

1669 Appointed Professor of Mathematics

1696 Revised coinage of the country

1703 Elected President of the Royal Society

1671 Gave his reflector telescope to Royal Society

In ...1665 I found the Method of approximating series ... and ... the method of Tangents ... the next year ... the Theory of Colours ... . And the same year I began to think of gravity ... All this was in the two plague years of 1665–1666. For in those days I was in the prime of my age for invention & minded Mathematics & Philosophy ...

Source E   The Royal Observatory (1675–6)

What is the Royal Society?

Some scientists formed a society where they could share their knowledge and carry out experiments. It is called the Royal Society and it still exists today. King Charles II supported it, and granted it a **charter** in 1662. Members of the Royal Society were interested in many areas of science. For example, Sir Christopher Wren was not only an architect (page 71), he was also a mathematician, astronomer and inventor. Robert Hooke was a clever scientist who wrote a book describing the experiments he had carried out using his microscope. Samual Pepys, who recorded the events of the Plague and the Great Fire of London in his diary, was also a member of the Royal Society (pages 66–71).

Astronomy

Charles II set up the Royal Observatory at Greenwich to study, measure and record the positions of the stars and the movements of the planets and the moon. He made John Flamsteed the Astronomer Royal. In 1682 an astronomer called Edmond Halley (1656–1742) saw a comet in the sky. He worked out that the comet's path round the sun meant that it would only be seen every 76 years. Halley made the first 'map' of the stars in the southern sky. He also built a diving bell to help find out about the world under the sea.

Investigations

1 The letters A and B in Source **C** show the benefits of Newton's telescope. What were they?

2 Newton said he had reached his peak as a mathematician in 1665-6. How old was he in 1666? Where and when did Newton make his most important discoveries?

3 Who set up the Royal Observatory? When was it set up, and for what purpose?

4 The room is called the 'Star Room' (*Cameram Stellatam*). Why do you think this was? How can you tell that the observatory was used to observe, record and measure the position of the stars and the movement of the planets and the moon?

5 The seventeenth century is called the age of the scientific revolution. Using the information in this chapter can you say why?

Key words

Charter   A written paper granting rights by the monarch.

# Index